PEOPLE OF THE POTLATCH

NATIVE ARTS AND CULTURE OF THE PACIFIC NORTHWEST COAST

VANCOUVER ART GALLERY WITH THE UNIVERSITY OF BRITISH COLUMBIA

PREFACE

This publication is designed to serve two purposes: first as a handbook to a very important exhibition of Pacific Northwest Indian art and secondly as an addition to the somewhat sparse publishing in this field.

The exhibition was organized in the Spring of 1956 by the Vancouver Art Gallery in co-operation with the University of British Columbia. From the many hundreds of objects included, a careful selection was made for reproduction in this book. In choosing this material we attempted to show as wide a range of the art form as space permitted, bearing in mind the desirability of selecting as many objects as possible of high quality which had not previously been published elsewhere.

Whilst Pacific Northwest Indian art has been studied carefully by many devoted people, most of their documentation is not readily available to the public in usable form. It is therefore hoped that this handbook will find its greatest usefulness in spreading knowledge of this very rich culture.

Special thanks for advice and technical assistance are due to Dr. H. Hawthorn, Curator, Museum of Anthropology, University of British Columbia; Mr. Wilson Duff, Anthropologist, Provincial Museum Victoria; Mr. Thomas C. Colt Jr., Director, Portland Art Museum; Dr. Erna Gunther, Director, Washington State Museum; Dr. Wayne Suttles, Department of Anthropology, University of British Columbia; Mr. Robert Hume, Vancouver Art Gallery staff; and finally Mrs. Audrey Hawthorn, Associate Curator, Museum of Anthropology, University of British Columbia, who has worked with me, stage by stage, throughout the whole project.

J. A. MORRIS,
Curator,
Vancouver Art Gallery.

LENDERS TO THE EXHIBITION

We are deeply grateful to the following for their generous loans.

Dr. C. E. Borden, Department of Anthropology, University of British Columbia

City Museum, Vancouver

Clayton W. McCall, Vancouver

Museum of Anthropology, University of British Columbia

Portland Art Museum

Provincial Museum, Victoria

William Reid, Vancouver

Mrs. Evelyn Lipsett Ryan, Vancouver

Washington State Museum, Seattle

PEOPLE OF THE POTLATCH

by *Audrey Hawthorn*

Associate Curator, Museum of Anthropology, University of British Columbia

THE PEOPLE OF THE NORTHWEST COAST

The sea was the source of life to the Indians of the Northwest Coast. Their villages were oriented to it; food was sought within its depths and along its shoreline. The waters of the sea were the familiar highways they travelled in their strong canoes.

Of all the products of the sea, salmon was the most eagerly sought. Abundance of salmon determined the pattern of all life; the elaborate ceremonial and social entertainments so important to the people of this region were made possible by the surplus of dried and smoked fish which could be stored for the future. Abundance of salmon meant that hard work during the fishing season could provide months of leisure, time for everyone to enjoy the vivid dramas and entertainments of the winter ceremonies.

As salmon was the basic food, so was cedar basic to the material culture invented by the people of this coast. The clean, easily-worked grain of the cedar made it the most versatile of materials. From the wood itself Indian craftsmen produced large houses, strong canoes, domestic utensils and massive carvings, as well as elaborate equipment for dances and dramas. From the rootlets of the cedar came a never-ending variety of baskets and textiles.

Over a span of generations the Indians of the Northwest Coast devised an intricate culture, built primarily on cedar and the salmon. From this foundation evolved a society as colourful and dramatic as any of the non-literate cultures of the world.

People of the Northwest Coast lived in small villages scattered along the rugged, indented coastline for a thousand miles from Alaska to northern California. From the north to the south there were gradations and differences of habit, idea and custom, but it was language which distinguished one group from another. They spoke many different languages, all of which were mutually unintelligible, and for this reason we set apart each group speaking a distinct language as a "tribe", although such a tribe had no political bonds.

There were seven different groups or tribes in this Northwest Coast region, who shared a similarity of culture. In the north lived the *Tlingit* and *Tsimshian* tribes. The *Haidas* inhabited the Queen Charlotte Islands. On the west coast of Vancouver Island lived the *Nootka* people, while the *Kwakiutl* occupied northern Vancouver Island and the adjacent mainland.

From the mouth of the Fraser River and southward down the Washington Coast were the *Coast Salish:* some divisions of these people also lived on the southern portion of Vancouver Island.

There were, perhaps, 50,000 people within these tribes, living on the coastline at the end of the 18th century. Over a period of mutual history they had travelled from one place to another to visit, to inter-marry, to wage warfare and to take slaves. They had traded products and had borrowed from each other many customs and ideas. This interchange of people, ideas and materials resulted in a culture which was similar for the whole Northwest region. Differences there were and divergencies of many kinds, but so much of

their way of life was similar, that we speak of them all as "the people of the Northwest Coast".

EARLY CONTACTS WITH WHITE CULTURE

Among the tall cedars, along the rocky sea coast, the first men arrived. Of the years and circumstances of their travels we know but little. They left only traces of themselves; tools of stone and bone and fragments of their beliefs carved into stone.

How many generations passed, in the mists and the rainfall of this coast land, as they learned the methods of living comfortably here! Only the archeologist can disclose to us the process of this long adjustment. From the material fragments of culture left behind, some of their story can be reconstructed.

By the time the European explorer became aware of the people on the Northwest Coast, it was already late on our European calendar. It was the end of the 18th century before travellers converged on this region — the Spaniards in 1774, Captain Cook from England in 1777, others following soon after in greater frequency. By 1778 the English had established the first trading post at Nootka and in 1799 the Russians founded Sitka. Regular trade routes and contacts were organized for the purpose of collecting the lustrous sea-otter pelts which could be sold so profitably in the markets of Europe and the Orient.

Within the hundred years that followed, the culture of the Northwest Coast flowered in elaborate profusion. Artistic and social development reached a peak of achievement. Richly creative, unique among the cultures of the world, it nevertheless collapsed at the end of the century, overwhelmed by disintegrating forces.

Traffic was brisk between the European traders and the Indians. Fur pelts were desired for the Eastern markets and the trader had much that the

Indian could use to advantage. Muskets became a necessary part of a man's hunting gear. With firearms, more furs and a greater food supply could be procured with less effort. Steel knives and axes quickly replaced the stone and bone blades of pre-trade days. The efficiency of carving with steel resulted in a new profusion of totem poles, more complexly carved and in a whole array of new wooden ceremonial articles. New trade goods were eagerly sought as the glossy pelts piled high on the counter. Traders brought in woven blankets, which the women quickly adapted to ceremonial use, trimming them with bright red cloth and shell buttons. Sheet copper came in for the rich to buy as display wealth.

Trade and contact brought, however, more than goods and a new standard of living. Settlement and the musket upset the balance of animal-human life; animals for fur and food became harder to find. Newly-dependent on the goods of the store, involved in a complex pattern of spend-ing lavishly for hospitality and in debt for this pattern, the Indian was forced to work for money and on terms dictated by the White culture. A routine of life which had been satisfactory to individuals over many generations was disrupted in response to the new conditions.

Alcohol, used as a trade item, contributed to family disintegration and demoralization. The ravages of disease for which no immunity had been established increased these effects; smallpox and measles swept uncontrolled along the coast. Whole villages were suddenly depleted by death and by flight, large families were reduced overnight to insignificance.

As a final blow to the old culture, the potlatch was banned by the Federal Government in an effort to hasten the adjustment of the Indian to White Canadian culture. The potlatch, with its emphasis on family prestige and social position, with its extravagant hospitality and widespread credit sys-

tem, was at the very core of Indian culture. When it was forbidden, so was the whole way of life which had given it meaning. Native life was halted in one of its primary means of expression. Missionaries increased the doubts and conflicts which individuals felt about their disintegrating world; each person groped to find a new meaning, a new way of expressing life, in the midst of this end-century chaos.

Fortunately for us of a later generation, there were people concerned with recording this old culture before it disappeared forever. From the records made by such people, we can get a picture of the richness and meaning of a way of life different from our own, and can value it and the people who invented it.

Our most detailed knowledge comes from the anthropologist Franz Boas, who began work on the Northwest Coast in 1886, and over a period of years collected the memories and technical knowl-edge of a great number of the people who had grown up in the old days. The anthropologist-photographer Edward Curtis, arriving in the first decade of the 20th century, sought out people to pose for characteristic activities and scenes. Explorers such as Niblack and Emmons, attached to the U. S. Navy, spent years in collecting the material culture representing these people and made themselves experts whose collections were sought by the great museums of the world.

The Northwest Coast, indeed, was in danger of losing much of its material culture as collectors, artists and museums competed for examples of the outstanding art forms. It is fortunate that, while there was yet time, the Province took steps to establish a policy of retaining at least some of this much-desired material. Dr. C. F. Newcombe amassed a splendid collection for the Provincial Museum at Victoria.

The Province was fortunate, moreover, in having a

few far-sighted individuals who devoted much time, energy and money to illustrating and preserving the material life of the Northwest Coast Indians. Dr. G. H. Raley, on this coast since 1884 as a United Church missionary, is an outstanding representative of this group. There are others, too, who have enriched museums and galleries with their collections.

THE PATTERN OF THE YEAR

The people of the Northwest Coast met each new season with a change of occupation and of place, giving life a welcome variety.

In the spring, people left the confinement of the big houses and went to the beaches and to nearby fishing grounds. Early spring brought great migrations of salmon and eulachon up the rivers, when the Nass, the Skeena, the Fraser and many smaller streams ran thick with swarms of spawning fish. Men and women, too, travelled to the places which were allocated to them by inheritance for the

fishing. Men caught the fish with weirs, nets, traps and by use of gaffs, spears and hooks, while women prepared the large catches for immediate and for future use. Eulachon was especially valued for its rich oil, which was rendered out by the women into large tubs or canoes.

Spring brought with it a welcome variation of diet and new activities directed toward procuring it. Women and children searching for new vegetable foods found pleasure and change in these food gathering expeditions.

Summer increased the freedom of travel, of work and of housekeeping. Families often left the village entirely and pitched summer camps near the best fishing sites. Here each family owned the right to a special spot from which its men fished, while the women worked in family or household groups to preserve large catches for the future. This was a pleasant time of year, for the assiduous work was accompanied by the pleasures of visits,

gossip and the relaxations of housekeeping. It was also a crucial time of year, for it was the abundance of fish gathered now which insured the leisure time and the life of hospitality which was looked forward to for the winter months.

In late summer people had time to travel more freely. Friends and relatives could visit other villages, or could entertain visitors, offering some of the surplus food as hospitality. This season saw some of the most lavish of the big feasts, when whole families had garnered enough food not only for the entertainment of large numbers of guests, but also for presentation as gifts. It was a good time for trading, too. With the abundant produce from the summer's work, men loaded their canoes and travelled to traditional meeting places on the coast. At such points men from many tribes gathered; tribes far inland, north and south, all converged to trade. These visits resulted in the exchange of many products and of new ideas.

With the onset of the rainy winter months, members of the household groups returned to their permanent villages and took shelter in their large cedar houses. It was then that social life became most colourful and dramatic, for this was the time in which the secret societies took over the life of the village. The supernatural beings of the spirit world came down to initiate the young and to dramatize for the elders the compelling and traditional ways of the spirits who influenced human life and history. While gales and slanting rains dominated the outside world, the spirits in vivid costumes and startling masks re-enacted the myths and legends of the early world. The audience sat enthralled, caught up into a world of imagination and recreation, of colour and movement and rhythm.

WOMEN AND DAILY LIFE

Women who were not slaves had a full and pleasant life. They could inherit family titles and privileges and could bring wealth and honour to their hus-

bands. They could, on occasions, rise to positions of chieftainship and high social rank.

Daily life was not too arduous and women of a household could share the routine in company. Women took charge of small children, they prepared and preserved the food, they gathered foods to supplement the staple diet provided by the men and they wove the textiles, made the mats, basketry, twine and string.

In company with others, women and their small children made forays along the beach in search of shellfish and seaweed; they went into the meadows for camas lily bulbs and clover roots and into the fields for berries. Other days they made expeditions into the forest for the long cedar rootlets which were used for weaving baskets. When textiles were to be woven bark must be gathered and shredded, or in the case of the coloured Chilkat blankets, wool must be gathered or plucked, spun and dyed. Basketry and weaving could both be done as occasional work while gossiping, or could be worked at intensively over a period of time. Little girls learned early to imitate the domestic skills of their mothers.

On the occasion of an expedition to the family fishing grounds, women worked hard in preparing the fish for storage but they also enjoyed the freedom of a change away from the usual household routine. At these times they prepared the fresh fish as the catch came in, filleting it and smoking or sun-drying it on large racks.

Ordinary cooking involved a variety of methods, boiling being the most usual. Hot stones were added to a wooden or basketry vessel containing water and, as the water boiled, the fish or meat was thrown in. Baking was done in an earthen pit lined with hot stones and seaweed. Fish, meat and vegetable roots were roasted or steamed in this manner. A third variation was an open fire-barbecue over which a split fish or piece of meat

was balanced on skewers. Fish oil was regarded as a condiment and accompanied most foods for seasoning. Meals were generally served on a cedar-bark mat placed on the floor. Each person had an individual dish and spoon, with a serviette of shredded cedar bark. Rules of etiquette restricted the manners of all; for example, young girls must never take large mouthfuls, must chew daintily and must keep the eyes lowered. Men must not drink water during a meal and could eat only certain parts of the fish in a certain manner.

MEN'S ACTIVITIES

Men had a variety of pursuits and responsibilities, the chief of which was to provide the main food supply. Fish was the staple and its pursuit took much of a man's time and ingenuity. All the main varieties of the sea and the river were sought; salmon, herring, cod, halibut, eulachon, smelts varied in favour. These were taken in many ways with traps, weirs, dams, nets, harpoons and many types of hooks. Canoes were used for sea fishing. In rivers fish were often netted and speared from specially-built platforms, each owned by a family as an inherited property.

Hunting was subsidiary to fishing as a source of food. In general the sea people did not care for hunting in the deep forest. Although deer, bear and mountain goat were occasionally hunted for their meat with traps and deadfalls, sea mammals were preferred to the animals of the forest. Sea lions, seals and porpoises were sought for their flesh and their fur was used as a by-product.

The whale was eaten in some places when it was available, as when one was stranded on the beach. But among the Nootka of the west coast of Vancouver Island, the pursuit of the whale was an admirable and glorious quest. Only a chief could head a whaling expedition and all the men who were to accompany him went through ordeals of starvation and sleeplessness to acquire special

power. When they went out in the long canoe each man knew his station in the boat and his special duties. A whale hunt might involve following the monster out into the open sea for several days. A successful capture was a triumphal occasion in the village, with offerings made to the whale spirit to placate him.

Besides hunting and fishing each man was responsible for the production of the daily utensils, tools and gear used by his family and in his own work. Wood was split and planed for boxes, dishes or seats, and stone or bone tools were split and ground into shape. The production of major carpentry such as fine boxes, totem poles, canoes and houses was left to specialists.

The hunting of fur animals was another occupation of the men. Both sea and forest animals were sought for their pelts and were captured in the same manner as the animals sought for food—by the use of traps, deadfall, bow and arrow in the forest, and by use of the harpoon in the water. Originally the furs were used as cloaks by the chiefs and as household robes and bedding, but after the advent of the trader furs were sought as trade goods and procuring them occupied more time. Men also had the responsibility of gathering wealth for potlatch use and for the repayment of social debts. By astute trading a man could accumulate goods for this purpose. Members of many tribes met at traditional junctures to exchange fish oil, dried fish, shell jewellery, slaves and dried meat. Many of the overland paths travelled by traders on foot are still discernible and, because of the principal item of trade, are called "grease trails".

Warfare was occasionally undertaken, always as a small localised skirmish between household groups or villages of different tribes. War was decided upon for several reasons: for revenge of some slight or insult against a family or village, for retaliation or for procuring slaves. In any case, the men of a

household or a village group would confer as to whether to undertake the project and the shaman was consulted for his predictions and prophecies. If it was decided that the outcome seemed good, both the men and the women of the household or village group undertook various rituals and prayers to ensure success. All preparations were made as quietly and secretly as possible, for swift surprise was the essence of success. The canoes were launched amid the prayers of the village and the warriors travelled by night, as dawn was the preferred time of attack. If the attack was for purposes of revenge, women and children were not spared: if slaves were sought, they were taken captive. Villages involved in warfare were constantly on the alert. Some were located on cliffs commanding a wide view with defense in mind. Houses in these villages were constructed with a narrow entrance admitting only one person at a time to prevent a surprise attack. However, warfare and crisis with other groups were exceptional and most of life was lived within the peaceful confines of daily village routine.

During the greater part of the year there was time for leisure and recreation.

Sports of several kinds were played along the beaches by men and boys. There was a stick game in which a long stick was used to secure a small round perforated stone. A form of shinny was played with teams knocking a ball to a goal with crooked clubs. In some regions canoe-racing competitions were held, using specially-constructed light canoes for the purpose. Wrestling and feats of strength such as tug-of-war were popular.

Guessing games were everywhere prevalent. In a typical game participants were divided into teams, one team holding marked bones, while the other team guessed where they were located or which sticks were held. Other gambling games involved the use of dice, and tally sticks were used

to keep score. Excitement ran very high as one side adopted tactics intended to confuse the team which was guessing. Tension often kept the game going for long hours at a time.

Informal recreations included sitting and talking while whittling small objects, such as toys for the children. For both men and women life held a reasonable balance of work and recreation, and a man's whole life was interwoven with the lives of his household and his village.

THE CORE OF THE CULTURE

Every society has its own particular flavour, composed of the special attitudes, beliefs, customs and ideas by which that society lives. The following is an attempt to present the basic core of beliefs and customs which characterized the culture of the Northwest Coast.

In the beginning, all living things shared the world in a state of equality and mutual understanding. Animals, birds, fish, men—all had the same types of motives and wishes. They all spoke or were able to understand the same language; indeed the main difference between them was in their superficial external appearance, birds with beaks and feathers, animals with fur, fish with scales. If for convenience or comfort this body covering were removed, the form underneath was indistinguishable from human form. This fact, of course, led to great confusion. A human being lured under water was invited to live in the country of the Salmon People and after many years returned to his own people with the secrets, techniques and lore learned from his sojourn below. Or a woman might be married to a stranger and later learn that he was a bear. From him she learned various secrets and powers which she handed on to her own people. Variations on these mistakes in identity were elaborate and numerous.

Characters in Northwest Coast legends often had

personalities which led them into special escapades. Raven, for example, was full of curiosity and mischief. Often his adventures benefited mankind inadvertently, as when he discovered fire or released the moon to shine in the sky. Killer Whale, Salmon, Frog Woman, Bear, Wolf, Eagle and many others were individuals who acted in an endless chain of adventures, as a result of which lessons were learned by mankind. Special ways of behaviour and of treating others were remembered by each descendant of these illustrious original characters. The people who claimed descent from them inherited certain symbols as reminders of the early history—a mask, a staff, or a special dance, together with the appropriate legend.

Another facet of the belief in man-and-animal origin was that man was totally dependent on the goodwill of the animals which he used for food and must, therefore, propitiate and please them. Many legends were concerned with teaching this lesson.

One member of a community, cruel to an animal or fish, caused the whole community to suffer. When young boys tormented the Salmon people, swimming up-river, all the Salmon were grieved and indignant and swam away, never to come again near that place. Related to the legend, many rituals and taboos were observed in the use of food. For example, on the occasion of the early salmon run, special rites and celebrations were directed toward the first salmon caught, which must always be cut with a certain type of knife, filleted a certain way and all the bones thrown back into the water where they would be re-formed. Other legends taught rewards for kindness and helpfulness toward animals. Many were the tales of help accorded a stranger who turned out to be an animal and returned the aid in time of need.

All these heroes of myth and legend might be ancestors from whom many properties were inherited. Special stories, masks, costumes, songs and

dances related to these early days were regarded as heirlooms and as jealously guarded as other inheritances. In addition to these dramatic bequests were the noble names by which an ancestor was known, the crests and emblems of his person and the special privileges he acquired or invented. Ancestors with their property, and other property in addition, could be acquired through judicious marriage, or through successful warfare, and sometimes through audacity by laying claim to another's special property without retaliation.

This complex of heroic ancestors, their bequests to future descendants and stories about human behaviour were all interwoven into the fabric of everyday life. Genealogy, with an emphasis on inheritance, was a paramount fact, constantly referred to. Rivalry for status, employing wealth for this purpose, was a pervasive factor in all life on the Northwest Coast. The potlatch, with its emphasis on family, inheritance and display, and the winter ceremony, with its recounting of legends of the time of creation, were both deeply rooted in these beliefs.

On looking at the material culture of these people, one realizes that family crests are everywhere displayed and repeated. The front of the cedar house is painted with the family crest; usually a totem pole before the door commemorates both ancestors and special incidents. Inside, carved house posts continue the display of heraldic symbols. The settee used as a seat by the chief and his wife is painted with a crest and so are the storage boxes, the food dishes and spoons. Other family insignia adorn the ceremonial clothing, the painted hats, canoe prows and many other articles of both daily and ceremonial life.

Each individual was born into a clan, determined by the clan into which father or mother, or both,

were born. (This reckoning varied with tribes and with regions.) Clan members were descendants of one ancestor and claimed the emblem representing him; Raven, Bear, Wolf and Thunderbird are a few of the clan founders. All members of a clan were considered to be related and in most of these societies members of the same clan were forbidden to marry. In some northern regions each village was divided into several clans, providing a convenient, practical division for purposes of marriage and various social services. Rivalry was established between the men of the clans for athletic contests and between all for games and hospitality.

The most important feature of Northwest Coast life was its system of social ranking. At the top were the chiefs and their wives, each chief being the head of a household. In the large house four or five or more families shared living space and the fortunes of the household. Some chiefs wielded more power and importance in village affairs by virtue of their descent, their success in potlatching, or by their wisdom. Those who lived with the chief comprised the household and usually belonged to the middle ranks of the society. Although these people might have claim to illustrious ancestors, they had not potlatched their way to high rank. They shared the honour and prestige of a great chief and so were industrious in co-operating with him when he wished to gain more rank and status.

The people at the bottom of the social system were the slaves. Taken in war or trade, they did the menial chores of the household and were at the mercy of their owners.

All the people of the Northwest Coast believed in the importance of social rank and status as the regions of man's deepest striving. Rank, privilege, aggrandizement—these were the worthy goals of man's effort.

THE POTLATCH

All striving for status was directed through one channel, the potlatch. It was the means through which a man claimed his right to his ancestral inheritance, made good his claim by proving it and so established a higher position for himself in public opinion. The potlatch was basic to all Northwest Coast social life. Involved in it were three essential ideas:

1. All important claims or occasions should be celebrated publicly.

2. Witnesses must be invited to observe that everything was conducted with all proper procedure. These witnesses must be paid.

3. All guests must be hospitably entertained. This entertainment and the payment of the guests were an index of the wealth and resources of the host.

Many events could be the excuse for the giving of a potlatch. The introduction of a small child to the village, the coming of age of a daughter or a nephew, a death, a marriage, or simply the assumption of a new name or title which had not been previously claimed. Sometimes several events were celebrated at once.

A potlatch could not be announced until much wealth had been garnered and stored. Since the status and prestige of the whole household was at stake, all would co-operate in planning and gathering the amount necessary. To gather all that would be needed for hospitality and for gift distribution might take months, even years. All debts that were owed by other persons were called in for payment as well. The household playing host needed to have a superabundance of food, for the invited guests had to be fed for as long as the ceremonies should last. Several hundred visitors might arrive to attend a potlatch and might stay for several weeks.

There must be ample gifts to distribute among the witnesses. Gifts were ranked in importance: to rival chiefs would be given the valuable canoes, carved chests, slaves and fine clothing, while at the other end of the social scale, small strips of blankets were a token payment. A careful accounting was kept of each gift and to whom it went, for these potlatch distributions were at the basis of Northwest Coast economy. Each gift or its equivalent was *owed* back to the giver and was to be paid back within a stated interval, plus a definite rate of interest. In some cases the value to be returned was a 100% increase. This made for a system of circulating credit on which a man could count, calling back his wealth in due time. It was also an insurance system, for payment was owed to the heirs of a deceased man in his stead, or conversely was owed *by* the heirs of a debtor. For a man to fail in his obligations was unthinkable.

When a man owed a number of rival chiefs, he too began to plan a potlatch, at which time he would not only discharge his debts, but also attempt to be even more lavish in the gifts which he returned.

This social rivalry was epitomised among the Kwakiutl in the display of the "Copper". This was a sheet of copper in the form of a shield which represented a great unit of wealth. Each copper had a name bestowed on it, reminiscent of the amount of wealth which had been paid for it. Its display at the ceremony was a dramatic event and sometimes in the heat of demonstrating his great wealth, claimed as beyond that of any other chief present, the owner would break the copper into pieces. This was a challenge to other chiefs to be able to do likewise.

The potlatch itself was a colorful and complex affair. A messenger summoned guests from the related villages. Wearing their finest ceremonial clothing, guests arrived in their canoes and were welcomed on the beach with songs and dances. After being installed within the village households,

everyone was summoned by a messenger to the house of the potlatch, where each was seated according to rank. An orator, dressed in his finery with an orator's staff of special carving, stood beside the chief and spoke for him, welcoming all, thanking them for coming and summarising the occasions to be celebrated.

For a period of days, depending on the events to be signalized, the guests were entertained by the dramatic recitations and dances celebrating family history. Members of the family, in masks and costumes, re-enacted the legends on which inheritance claims were based. Sometimes several kinds of events at once would be introduced, explained and witnessed. Each day found the crowd being fed; from the elaborate feast dishes food was served out with great ladles into smaller-sized group dishes and then served into still smaller ones for each person. The people were exhorted to eat well for the host's sake, as there was so much food at hand.

Many of these potlatches featured the raising of a totem pole carved specially to commemorate the occasion. Amid speeches of explanation and rejoicing, the heraldic pole was raised to stand by the house as a tangible reminder of the potlatch.

On the last day the gifts would be called out, displayed and given to the assembled guests, while the orators stressed the wealth and lavishness of the host. Guests dispersing from the potlatch took away with them not only gifts, but detailed discussion of the occasion. They recounted to their villages the success of the potlatch and of the host's claims. If all had gone well, the host henceforth could freely use his new claims and add new emblems to his costumes and carvings. Even although temporarily bankrupted, if he had surpassed rival chiefs the wealth expended was worthwhile and in any case was owed him and his household for a future return.

The potlatch stimulated all the arts. Gifts made for the occasion, carved boxes, canoes, dishes, jewelry, mats, baskets, must be of the finest. The ceremonial blankets and headgear worn by both guests and the hosts were elaborately made and valuable. The totem pole was critically appraised and the best carver available had been engaged to carve it. Oratory, dances and songs were likewise stimulated, old forms improved upon and new ones invented.

When the potlatch was banned by the Government the blow struck deep into the structure of Northwest Coast society. Without the potlatch much of the creative effort given to the costume, regalia, performance, and even the value given to the gathering of wealth, became meaningless.

WINTER CEREMONIES AND THE SECRET SOCIETIES

As the winter months set in, as the nights grew cold and the dark came early, the village waited expectantly the call of ghostly whistles in the woods. In this way the supernatural spirits announced their presence in the village; from now on for the next few months ordinary life was at a standstill. Now the supernatural spirits came down to instruct the young and to show to all the traditions and legends of the spirit world. There were many kinds of spirits, each incorporated into a society with its own legends, costumes and its own place in the scale of social ranking.

Some of the societies were those of the great bird monsters who lived on the top of a remote mountain and ate human flesh; of the double-headed dragon whose appearance betokened wealth; of the frightening cannibal woman of the forests whose cry, when heard in the woods, meant good luck. Membership in the secret societies was regarded as an honor and a young person was the center of attention when he was chosen to be

a novice in one of them. For a time he was kept in seclusion, often fasting as an ordeal. He was taught the ways of his society, how to do its dances, sing its songs and observe its ritual. When he was rehearsed, a special dance was held in which he was introduced, sometimes dramatically, as when he jumped down through a hole in the roof and raced through the house. (Usually at this time, as if he were in the throes of a seizure, he acted out a form of being affected by the spirits, and behaved in an aberrant fashion.) Each stage of his initiation had its own proper form of dancing and other behavior. Gradually his fellow members showed him how to control the spirit within him and to return to human society. After his singing and dancing showed that he had become a full-fledged member of the group, a potlatch was often given by an uncle to pay the members of his society who had successfully carried through his initiation.

Stage managing for these ceremonies was complicated and dramatic. Novices disappeared under-

ground in a flash, into nowhere—through concealed underground passages. Voices were heard from nowhere and from everywhere—through concealed speaking tubes. Mock fights appeared to be fatal —with the deft use of concealed bladders of blood and false portrait heads carved of wood. Impressive supernatural figures in costumes and masks concealing human appearance danced around the room, lit only by the flames of a central fire. In the background whistles made a haunting cry, as the drums gave the beat of the dancers and their songs. To this rhythm the dancer, sometimes crouching, sometimes springing, danced slowly around the square of the fire, imitating the motions of the spirit, bird or animal, which he represented. At each corner of the square in turn he stopped and danced in a small square. This pattern was repeated four times. At intervals others might follow and using the same rhythm and pattern go likewise around the fire four times. Soon the whole room would be filled with these figures from

the animal and spirit world, turning, posturing, dancing in the light of the fires.

THE ART OF THE NORTHWEST COAST

In looking at a display of things made by people of the Northwest Coast, one cannot help being impressed by the tremendous vitality of the culture and of its expression in a strong traditional art form. Wherever the eye rests there is an object of interesting shape, of technical complexity and of a delightful finish. What a profusion of material! Finely carved boxes of wood, delicate horn spoons, intricate carvings of ivory, dramatic patterns in woolen textile — all these articles are stamped with a sincerity of purpose, an emotional concern that gives them a living meaning to us now. Even though the culture that created them is gone, we still feel the impact of their vitality as art forms.

The art of the Northwest Coast Indians was a bold and vivid art pervading all of life. The animal forms that decorated their objects were familiar and important forms to them. Ancestral heroes who helped found the history of man, animal beings who helped to invent and teach new ways, family heroes who showed bravery or cunning in a crisis and made their descendants proud to claim them— these were given tangible pictorial form and were repeated endlessly as the themes of family and ceremonial life. Killer-whale for example appears on a painted hat, on an appliqued robe, as a woven figure in a wool blanket, as a carved rattle, on a whistle, as a mask; he can be found on a carved box, on a totem pole, as part of a house post and on the handle of a horn spoon. These representations might not have been stirring, nor artistic, however, had it not been for two things.

First, the traditions of portraying these forms provided many techniques for carving and painting which gave the artist a wide choice of selection and at the same time set limits to his choice. A

traditional selection of a wide variety of possible forms and line arrangements gave him both familiarity and freedom in using the traditional symbols. In weaving, in carving, in painting, he created within a well-defined choice of symbols. Within the confines of these traditions and limits, he perfected methods which met very high creative standards.

The second factor which determined the level of artistic production was that the standards of technical craftsmanship were very high among all the people on the Northwest Coast. All men were expected to produce the tools and utensils used in daily life. Even for such simple objects the standards were high for symmetry, balance and finish. A glance at a stone hammer or an adze blade will show that the care expended on it is far beyond the demands of mere functional use. A man was expected to produce careful, well-made tools and utensils. All women wove baskets; learning the techniques for weaving at an early age, a woman took pride in the regularity and perfection of her weaving and decorated it for beauty's sake, not for mere utility: not to do so would put her outside standards of admiration and satisfaction that other women found. This emphasis upon fine craftsmanship determined that all the people who made things mastered the techniques needed in their production. A man who must make the daily food and storage boxes learned to make them well, solidly and handsomely. The control of the adze blade led to a freedom of use in employing it, so that a regular motion of the tool became the best method of finishing a wooden surface; hence the lightly rippled finish of so many pieces of carving.

Not all people were adept at all things; there were specialists in various crafts. A particularly experienced man would direct the construction of a plank house or the burning and steaming of a canoe. But beyond the specialists were the artists

who were recognized as skilled craftsmen, who had in addition an extra power.

This power could be inherited or it could be acquired, but it was a man with this power who was sought out for the carving of an important totem pole or an elaborate mask. His work was brought forth on an occasion when people would note and admire it and he was a valued and well-rewarded member of the community. Apprentices studying under him helped to spread his standards and techniques still further into the culture which was concerned with them.

The artist and the artisans, working within the traditional framework of their culture, spent much of their lives in creating and in producing material for daily and for ceremonial living. Working generation after generation they established the traditions of material and of technique, which we recognize as the distinctive art of the Northwest Coast.

SALIENT CHARACTERISTICS OF THE ART

The art of the Northwest Coast usually portrayed animal forms of legend and myth, each animal being characterized by a distinctive feature of anatomy. The Killer-whale may be recognized by a dorsal fin, a bifurcated tail and a blow hole. The beaver has two prominent front teeth, a cross-hatched broad tail and often appears holding a stick in two paws. The artist might represent the animal by these features alone instead of using the whole animal: whenever these characteristic symbols appear, the animal was intended.

Often the design form which represents the animal was expressed as if it were an X-ray picture. In this form the whole animal was constructed, inside as well as out, showing the pattern of spine, vertebrae and ribs, with joints and sockets shown in position.

There was a principle of intricate spatial relationships. The artist had a tradition of filling a space

with both lines and solid forms in a delicate balance, each enhancing the other. A ratio of line to space was established which seems perfect. The same principle was observed in the shaping of the design to the space to be covered. The carving of a columnar tree-trunk called for forms placed in a certain relationship to each other, as did the tapered handle of a carved horn spoon. The square sides of a wooden box were decorated in a different arrangement from that used in the decoration of a round hat with a high crown. The structure of the form, the design and the space were in perfect balance. It was usual for the artist to employ a variety of techniques for dividing space into interesting patterns and to produce variations of texture. The most common space-fillers were oval eye-forms, which were placed to indicate sockets and joints as well as used separately for points of punctuation and emphasis. Other space-fillers employed were parallel cross-hatched lines, a

curved line like a bracket and a form of round-cornered square.

This perfect balance of line, space and form is maintained in three-dimensional carving, which has a monumental quality. Whether in stone, ivory, bone or wood, a Northwest Coast carving is complete in its own proportions. A small detailed carving in ivory, such as a shaman's charm, could be reproduced on a scale many times its original size; the proportions and relationships would be so maintained that the perfection of form would be translated to monumental scale. On the same principle a huge totem pole could be reduced to the size of a pencil.

The section which follows is concerned with the materials and techniques used by the artists and craftsmen of the Northwest Coast and with the products they created. We cannot look at examples

of their work without being convinced that their culture offered to its participants a rich variety of creative outlets and the possibility of enduring personal satisfaction.

WOODWORKING

The men of the Northwest Coast were, foremost, workers in wood. A variety of woods were used for different purposes: yew, alder, maple, yellow cedar—but the most widely-used wood was the red cedar. Fine, even grain, easily split or carved, made this wood useful, as did its prevalence.

The houses and canoes were outstanding products of woodworking skill. The houses were large enough to shelter many people under one roof and were customarily lived in by four or five families. Of large cedar planks split from the living tree, they varied in size from about twenty by forty feet and ten feet high, to very large ones of several hundred feet and fifteen feet high, inhabited by many families. The walls were erected in a rectangle about a central structure of upright posts and roof-beams. The frame of the roof rested on these beams and was covered with cedar planks, with one or more moved aside so that smoke might escape. A large house might have a fire in every corner for individual families and one in the center. Often one or two tiers of wooden or earth platforms were raised around the four sides of the house, used for benches on which to sit, as platforms on which to sleep, or as shelves for the storage of household goods. The houses were built as a joint enterprise under the supervision of a specialist and at the commission of a chief. The completion of such a house was the occasion for a potlatch.

Canoes also were major undertakings, usually involving the efforts of several carpenters. The size varied according to the type of canoe needed, war canoes and those for whaling being larger and stronger than small family or river fishing canoes. The cedar log was selected, then hollowed out by

burning. Water was poured in and hot stones added to produce steam. The canoe was covered with a wet mat and the wood steamed until the sides could be made to flare by the use of struts, then the wood was allowed to dry and finished off by adzing smooth inside and out. A prow piece was added, which functioned as a harpoon rest and which also gave a graceful, flowing line to the curve of the canoe. Important canoes were carved and painted with the family crest emblem of the owner and such a canoe was a valuable possession.

Major carvings were made with the same set of tools used for small carvings: an elbow adze, a "D" adze, a curved knife and a chisel, with wedges for splitting. The most important carvings produced were totem poles, mortuary poles, house posts, chief's seats, carved boxes, large canoes, ceremonial masks, feast dishes and ladles, chief's ceremonial regalia, including rattles, headpieces and staff and a variety of ceremonial properties such as power boards, rattles, whistles and portrait masks.

As mentioned before, totem poles were the heraldic accounts of family history which were erected outside the door of the household. These poles were carved by a commissioned artist for the occasion of a potlatch. Traditions of carving these poles varied from region to region but all are monumental and impressive.

Mortuary poles were carved to hold and to honor the remains of a deceased chief. Often a beautifully carved box was placed atop the pole as his coffin; sometimes his remains were placed within a niche in a cross-beam between two poles.

The boxes produced by the carpenters were a triumph of woodworking technique. A cedar plank was grooved at three equidistant lines and then soaked in water for some days. With the application of heat the board was steamed until it could

be folded at the three groves to form the four sides of the box from one piece. The first and the fourth sides of the box were drilled with holes, through which a strip of cedar rootlet was threaded; the sides were then sewn together. A bottom was sewn on in similar fashion and the surface finished by adzing in parallel lines or by carving. The lid was often inlaid with shells. These boxes were much needed for storage of household effects, clothing and food, for use in canoe travel and for potlatch gifts. Small ones were often used as trinket boxes or workboxes for women, while others were carved with insignia for storing the effects of a shaman.

House posts, feast dishes and ladles were all ceremonial heraldic forms. The house posts bore one or more family crest animals and either two or four were fastened at the base of the four upright posts which supported the roof. Feast dishes were usually carved in the form of a crest animal or character and varied in size according to use.

Masks were of a variety and inventiveness not surpassed by any other mask-making people: there were masks for many occasions. Those worn by members of the secret societies, the bird-monster masks, are perhaps the most striking. The great long beaks are hinged so that at the pulling of a string, secretly concealed, beaks clack ominously. Other masks worn on ceremonial occasions depict various characters. One type representing an episode in legend reveals more than one character, being constructed in two or more sections which part on the pulling of a string to reveal another face inside. Some of the characters represented are highly stylized, so that it is impossible to guess without knowledge who is intended: others are so realistic as to be portraits of individuals and show the ability of the carver as an observer of reality as well as an inventor of fantastical images.

STONE CARVING

Archaeological deposits which have been excavated show that the ability to carve was evident from the earliest period of habitation. Stone tools were

beautifully worked; ivory and bone charms, pins and pendants were skillfully carved, often showing animal or human lineaments. How much wood might have been an element of these early cultures cannot be estimated since wood decays in the same surroundings in which stone and bone survive. Stone was a much used material. In general it was worked by pecking with another stone and then finished by grinding and polishing. Decoration was achieved by incising and carving out.

A number of pieces of stone figure carving have been dug up accidentally and at random on Vancouver Island and along the Fraser River. These are all affiliated in style and may be part of a whole regional stone carving tradition which extends down to the Columbia River region. The stones so far found are of two major types and have not usually been associated with other cultural materials.

Ranging from three inches high to twenty-three inches, are a number of carved bowls usually held by a human figure. Often the human features are finely delineated, with care taken to incise the face, headdress, spine and ribs. Sometimes a snake and a frog appear on the bowl. They probably had a ritual use. Found distributed over the same area as the above, a series of stone heads are also probably associated with shaman rituals. They are carved generally in a more perfunctory fashion, representing animal or human heads.

The carving of stone continued to more recent times. Mortars and bowls were often made of stone, some being used for the grinding of a native tobacco. Others were used to contain the earth ochres used in ritual face painting. In this case the bowl was often incised or carved into bird or animal form.

It is evident that there were a variety of stone tools devised before the advent of steel. Adze and chisel blades, knives and hammers were made by splitting

and grinding pieces of stone and polishing them with abrasives and water. The polishing process was continued until the objects were symmetrical, smooth and effective. A very interesting tool was a heavy-duty pounder used to drive fish-weir stakes into the river bed. For this, large square or triangular stones were polished, grooves being made for the thumbs. These hammers weighed fifteen or twenty pounds.

Greenstone or nephrite, found along the Fraser River, was traded over a wide area and blades from it were much desired. It was a smooth, translucent material, with much the same range of colouring as jade. A central core was cut into with an abrasive blade or saw, a parallel groove was then undercut, allowing a blade to be taken from the core which could be polished to a beautiful finish.

Small stone pipes were made and traded over a wide area. Some of these were straight, similar to our cigarette holders; others were fashioned to hold a hollow reed as a stem.

Occasionally stones were carved into forms which seem to have no functional reason and are not ceremonial: these we can simply call sculpture. One type is the stone totem poles which all seem to be recent and are very probably in the same class as the argillite carvings of this last century— tour-de-force carvings, to show skill and for fun. A few stone sculpture pieces are carved, apparently, for reasons of sheer creative artistry.

IVORY

The beautiful texture and color of ivory, as found in beaver or sea-lion teeth, seems to have attracted carvers from the earliest days. Usually it is found as a charm to be used by a shaman, either carried or worn as a pendant. An especially elaborate shaman's device, known as a "Soul-catcher", was a small beautifully carved ivory box with a removable stopper. This was used by the Shaman in capturing the wandering soul of a sick patient. These little boxes were often inlaid with abalone shell.

ARGILLITE

This is the shiny black, highly-polished stone found in the mountains near Skidegate, in the Queen Charlotte Islands. It is employed by the Haida Indians to carve elaborate *objets d'art*, small totem poles, candlesticks, plates and other items for modern decoration. Its use evolved during the last century to fulfil the demand for a portable, distinctive tourist souvenir. Many of the finest of the old Haida craftsmen devoted themselves to this work, enjoying the challenge of working in a new material and producing a number of spectacular objects. These are still in great demand but are increasingly hard to find.

BONE

Bone was used at times for the same purposes as ivory and was carved into shamans' charms, "soul-catchers", pendants, and into labrets and occasional ornaments. In addition, whale bone was used exten-

sively for the massive war clubs with carved heads which were in use at the time of Cook's arrival.

HORN

Delicate spoons were made of the small curved black horns of the mountain goat. By a process of steaming the horn and fastening it into a mould, a bowl was made, then the curved handle was carved into animals of the family crest. A beautiful spoon was much prized.

Occasionally horns of the mountain sheep were used in moulding a larger spoon and at times both types of horn were used on the same spoon, affording a pleasant contrast of color and texture.

OTHER CRAFTS

Metalwork was almost unknown in pre-contact days; the only metal used was a native copper which was traded down from the north. This usually

came in soft lumps and was treated simply by hammering into thin sheets. From these were made small ornaments; bracelets, nose and ear ornaments and gorgets. Small pieces may have been used to make an early form of "Copper" such as were used in the potlatch, but these did not become common until sheet copper was introduced. Copper sheathing from shipwrecked hulls may have been used, but it was the trader who imported a steady source of this commodity. This, too, was hammered into the ridges which form the "T" shape on the shield and was incised into a pattern with a sharp blade.

There is a possibility that iron could have preceded the White trader, since iron tools were reported at a very early date; shipwrecks could have yielded iron, as could barrels and boxes washed ashore. In any case, the virtues of iron as a blade were early seen and pieces of iron were hafted to form knives and adzes. Files which could be ground to a knife or dagger blade were important trade items.

The use of silver and gold coins as material for jewelry was adopted after contact with the Russian traders in Alaska and a new craft sprang up around it. A large coin was pounded to a long narrow strip and curved into bracelet form. This was incised with a sharp blade, using an over-all design of a traditional emblem. Bracelets of this sort were much valued by the women and made silver dollars an important trade item.

PAINTING

This craft had its own traditions and techniques, but usually existed as an adjunct to carving, embellishing and emphasizing forms already established in three dimensions.

Paint was applied for this purpose on most carved objects. Painting as an independent art, without carving, was done on house fronts and on the ceremonial backdrop curtains used in dramatic productions. The latter were sometimes large

woven mats, hung from the cross beams of the house, screening dressing rooms and behind-the-stage activities from the audience. After the introduction of cotton cloth, very large screens of unbleached muslin were used. The paintings of crests on these were often gigantic in concept and impressive in unity of design.

The woven hats made by the women were painted with crest designs in two or three colors. Men designed and painted the pattern boards which were copied by the women in weaving the intricate Chilkat blankets.

Before the days of commercially manufactured paints, colors were limited to the range of natural pigments which could be procured. Earth ochres of reds, browns and yellows were sought. A blue was made from copper oxide, or sometimes from blue clay. Black mud and charcoal were mixed to produce black, and white was obtained from the ashes of burnt clamshell. An oil base was mixed

with these for permanence, salmon eggs being preferred. Paints were used sparingly and did not weather very well out of doors. Totem poles of those days bear only faint traces of the paint which once brightened them. Indoor carvings fared better and the old paints imparted to the carved wood a rich, soft coloring. Red and black were perhaps the most frequently used colors. The introduction of store paint made possible a much wider choice and, since it was easily available, was more lavishly used.

BASKETRY

As the men of the Northwest Coast region were noted for their achievements as wood workers, so the women were famous for their production of baskets and textiles. A brief glance at the variety of baskets made by the women of this region shows a nearly endless variety of size, shape and purpose. Baskets were made for all types of domestic use, for gathering, storing and cooking foods of many

sorts. The same techniques were used to make hats and baby cradles.

Most of the basketry was woven from long, slender and pliant rootlets of cedar, or sometimes spruce. The only tool was a sharply pointed bone awl, which was used to split the rootlet into long strands for weaving and to bore a hole in which to insert the stitch. There were three basic variations of basketry stitches: 1. Coiling, in which a loop was wound around a core of fibres, becoming the base for the next stitch, eventually producing a parallel row, proceeding upward. 2. Twining, in which the strands of spruce or cedar were woven in and out of warp strands radiating from the bottom center of the basket. 3. Plaiting, in which warp and woof strands were woven simply in and out. Each of these techniques had many possible variations of size of warp in relation to woof strands, of stitch size and of spaces left open.

Each region had well-developed special traditions, which produced basketry characteristic of that area. Tlingit baskets are very fine, closely-woven twined spruce root, usually cylindrical in shape, often with lids. They were decorated with strands of maidenhair fern and grasses, dyed in natural colors. Haida baskets of twisted spruce root or cedar also were cylindrical or round and were commenced on a little hoop frame, starting with the bottom side up. Haida women also wove exceedingly fine crest hats of twisted spruce root. Kwakiutl women made several types of baskets, a specialty being a food basket of plaited open work, using strands of soft cedar bark. Salish women of the whole Fraser River area produced baskets of coiled cedar rootlet, which were decorated with an overstitch (imbrication) of red and black cherry bark and white bulrush. The variations of design produced by the placing of these colored stitches are very handsome. Nootka women, on the west coast of Vancouver Island and in some of the Puget Sound region, produced an extremely fine linen-like texture by weaving with narrow threads of bleached

swamp grass kept damp and pliable. Dyed grasses were used to produce a design against the white surface. Most of these small baskets were round or oval and had lids. They were much valued as trinket boxes.

WEAVING AND TEXTILES

Production of textiles by use of a loom was a rare technique among the Indian tribes of North America. The women of the Northwest Coast used the loom to weave three types of textiles. 1. The Chilkat blanket was woven by the women of the Tlingit tribe, of which the Chilkat tribe was one division. This type of heavy ceremonial robe was highly prized throughout the coastal region. The blanket was woven of mountain goat's wool, which was beaten and twined around a core of cedar bark twine. The woof was suspended from a single horizontal bar and the weft was twisted about each warp. Colors used to dye the goat's wool were pale blue, yellow and black, which were interspersed against the background of natural grayish-white. The design was contained in a five-sided form and consisted of crest symbols in intricate arrangement, surrounded by a broad margin of plain border. The bottom was terminated by a long, heavy fringe. The preparation and weaving of such a blanket might consume many months of a woman's time; the wool must be sheared, dyed, twined with cedar bark and strung, before weaving could even begin. The pattern of the blanket was copied from a board on which the pattern was painted, prepared by a man. 2. The Salish Blanket was woven by the Coast Salish women of the Georgia Strait and Puget Sound region. In early times the wool for this blanket was provided by a small woolly white dog, which was kept domesticated for the purpose of clipping. These dogs have been extinct now for many years. Dog wool was also combined with mountain goat's wool, fireweed fluff and small feathers. To these were added a white powdery clay and the whole was beaten with a stick to

make the fibres adhere to each other. All these fibrous substances were then spun into yarn and woven on a loom consisting of two upright posts holding two horizontal bars. After the traders arrived the blanket was sometimes decorated with strips of imported cloth or yarns of gay colors, which were entwined with other fibres to make a border of geometric pattern. These blankets were worn as a cloak over the shoulders by both men and women, and others were used as bedding. 3. A third textile, woven on the one-bar loom, was made of soft inner bark of the cedar tree, beaten to make it pliable and shredded into long strips. This was a most versatile form of material and was in general use for weaving the capes and skirts of everyday clothing worn by women, as well as mats, screens, blankets and sails. Well made mats were used as potlatch gifts and their production was part of a woman's general tasks.

CLOTHING

The wealthy chiefs and their wives wore fur cloaks. Sea otter pelts, soft and warm, were the most valuable, but other furs were also used. The skin was scraped, small pelts being sewn together with sinew or cedar twine through holes punched with an awl.

A cloak worn occasionally among the Salish and in the north was a robe of strips of fur and cedar bark twine, which had more strength and resilience than the cloaks of sewn skins. The tanning of hides was not a general practice on the Coast, such hides as were used being simply scraped and cleaned. In the more northern regions, people had contact with Interior tribes who tanned deer, moose and elk hides, wearing these as shirts, breeches and jackets. These were sometimes traded and worn by the Tlingit people, but in general, hide clothing was used only for occasional ceremonial purposes such as dance aprons. No moccasins were made or worn by the Indians of the Coastal region.

For everyday wear women wore skirts of woven cedar bark, or of shredded cedar bark fringe, sewn

together around the waist. Across the shoulders was worn a cedar bark blanket. Men ordinarily wore no clothing, save in rainy weather, when a cape of cedar bark was worn. Both men and women wore hats, which varied in style according to the region; Nootka people wore a bowl-shape hat, adorned by a small knob; people of the rest of the Coastal region wore hats with a high crown and flaring brim, often decorated with a painted crest pattern. A variation of this hat was worn on ceremonial occasions, when a chief would wear such a hat with the crown extended by woven rings, each ring indicating the number of his potlatch achievements. Among the northern tribes, such a hat was sometimes painted a solid color.

Ceremonial clothing was a complicated matter. On the introduction of the heavy blue Hudson's Bay Company blanket in mid-century, it was quickly adapted for ceremonial use. The women bought red flannel, with which they trimmed the border and appliqued a crest pattern on the center back.

This design and border were enhanced by the addition of cut pearl shell buttons used as outline. Most of these were trade buttons, though hand-cut shell ones were known. This same blanket and trimming were used to make crest shirts and dance aprons for ceremonial occasions.

With the blanket was worn a shirt or skirt and leggings. These latter might be fragments of Chilkat blanket weaving, or of deer hide, or simply of cloth. Shirts and skirts were sometimes woven specially by the Chilkat blanket weavers on the loom. These were trimmed with fur and were very valuable. The Chilkat blanket was the most prized item of ceremonial clothing to wear, surpassing the blue and red button blanket in value and appearance.

Headdresses were of several styles; the simplest was a ring of shredded cedar bark, dyed red with ochre. Such a ring was woven, twisted, or sewn, according to whether it represented the insignia

of a secret society or a clan. Sometimes it was decorated with white ermine and blue abalone shell. A neck ring of red cedar bark, denoting secret society rank, was also worn, each style determined by the society in which membership was claimed. Chiefs and women of rank wore a special headdress of a crest animal carved on a wooden plaque, mounted on a band worn around the head and adorned with long white ermine pelts. Such headdresses were very beautifully carved and inlaid with abalone. Chiefs carried, as part of their regalia, a rattle carved with a crest, which they would shake at some points in the oratory and dancing. They also carried staffs.

DANCE COSTUMES

The contrivance of costumes for the secret society dances, or for the dramatic performances of the potlatch, occupied much time and ingenuity and were regarded as heirlooms. Bear skins could be worn whole, while wolf and mountain goat suits used the real fur and wool covering. The mask worn over the head imitated the animal's appearance, concealing the human face. After the introduction of cotton cloth, it was possible to make a suit of cloth and to cover it with appropriate texture—feathers, fur, or burlap fringe simulating fur. In some dances only the mask was worn, the body being covered by a long fringe of shredded cedar bark, which left the arms and legs free.

Among the Salish different costumes were worn. Some of the tribes of Vancouver Island and of the mouth of the Fraser River had a dance in which the dancers wore a tunic of cloth, covered with parallel rows of black and white feathers. The associated mask was a carved wooden face with protuberant eyes and tongue, with nose and ears representing small animals. The mask was framed by a large stiff frill of bright cotton cloth, covering the head. Atop were sea-lion whiskers adorned with feathers. The dancers carried two rings of pecten shells. A spirit dance costume of the Coast Salish area was a dark cloth shirt or tunic, decorated with rows of

small carved paddles. A headdress of human hair was worn, representing a tall deformed head of olden days, embellished with long white feathers. Knees and ankles were encircled with rattles made of deer hoofs, which also rattled from a carved and painted staff which the spirit dancer carried.

JEWELRY

Before the advent of trade goods shell jewelry was much used. An early form of wealth was a series of small discs of cut shell, strung on a length of cedar bark or thong and worn as a necklace. This type of necklace has been found in early graves. Another type was composed of dentalium shells. These are slender, cylindrical shells, tapered at one end and were gathered from the rocky waters of the West Coast on a long pronged harpoon.

The most valued shell was that of the blue-green abalone, traded up from the California Coast. Pieces were standardized as to price, a square of three and one-half inches being worth twenty dollars. They were used as ear pendants, nose ornaments, gorgets and decorations sewn onto the button blankets. Pieces of abalone were used to embellish carvings of wood, ivory and bone.

In the north labrets were worn by women of rank, with size greater according to the rank of the wearer. Ear ornaments were worn by men as well as nose skewers and rings. Bracelets, anklets, ear ornaments and gorgets were made from native copper, which was hammered into thin sheets, then rolled. Brass, available later, was used in the same way.

After the introduction of silver and gold pieces by the traders, bracelets made of these metals became the most preferred ornament of the women. The hammered-out metal was also made into pins, pendants and ear rings and the bracelet, incised with a crest decoration, was almost an essential part of a woman's costume.

BODY DECORATION

Part of ceremonial adornment was the practice of painting the face and parts of the body with a symbol of one's crest. Sometimes this design was applied by hand, using a pigment of red or black earth mixed with oil. A special pattern form was carved to apply this crest design with precision on the face. The Haida made their crest designs permanent by tattooing them on arms, legs, or chests.

Head deformation was practised by several tribes, a specially built cradle holding the baby in place while soft pads pressed against its skull. The aim was to achieve a sloping forehead and an elongated crown.

USE OF NEW TRADE GOODS

It may be noticed that some pieces of Northwest Coast art are enriched with non-traditional materials. As artists, the Indians of the Northwest Coast were very quick to borrow any material or technique which might add to the beauty, splendour or impressiveness of their product. With this motive, they used all kinds of decorations—feathers, mirrors, embroidery, beads, thimbles; some of these materials became integrated (as the use of printed cotton fringe on some masks or the red and blue button blanket) and some did not. There was always an experimental approach toward new material.

PLATES

ALL OBJECTS ILLUSTRATED ARE LISTED BELOW BY PLATE NUMBER UNDER THE LENDER'S NAME.

DR. C. E. BORDEN, DEPARTMENT OF ANTHRO-
POLOGY, UNIVERSITY OF BRITISH COLUMBIA:
107

CLAYTON W. McCALL, Vancouver:
95

MUSEUM OF ANTHROPOLOGY, UNIVERSITY
OF BRITISH COLUMBIA:

PHOTOGRAPHS BY PETER HOLBORNE.

3, 5, 6, 7, 8, 9, 10, 11, 12, 13, 14, 17, 21, 22,
23, 25, 27, 29, 30, 32, 35, 36, 37, 38, 39, 40, 42, 43,
44, 45, 47, 50, 52, 53, 54, 55, 56, 57, 58, 59, 62, 63,
64, 67, 68, 71, 72, 75, 79, 83, 86, 87, 90, 91, 94, 96,
97, 98, 105

PORTLAND ART MUSEUM:
19, 89, 108

PROVINCIAL MUSEUM, VICTORIA:

1, 2, 4, 15, 16, 18, 20, 24, 26, 28, 31, 41, 51, 60, 61,
65, 66, 69, 70, 73, 74, 76, 78, 80, 82, 84, 88, 92, 93,
99, 100, 102, 103, 104, 106, 109

MRS. EVELYN LIPSETT RYAN, VANCOUVER:
46, 48, 49

WASHINGTON STATE MUSEUM, SEATTLE:
33, 34, 77, 81, 85, 101

SOME REFERENCES TO PLATES IN TEXT

2 CHILKAT BLANKET *TLINGIT* MOUNTAIN GOAT WOOL 52″ × 70″

4 CEREMONIAL BLANKET—BEAR *HAIDA* HUDSON'S BAY BLANKET DECORATED WITH RED FLANNEL AND PEARL BUTTONS 4½ x 5½ FT.

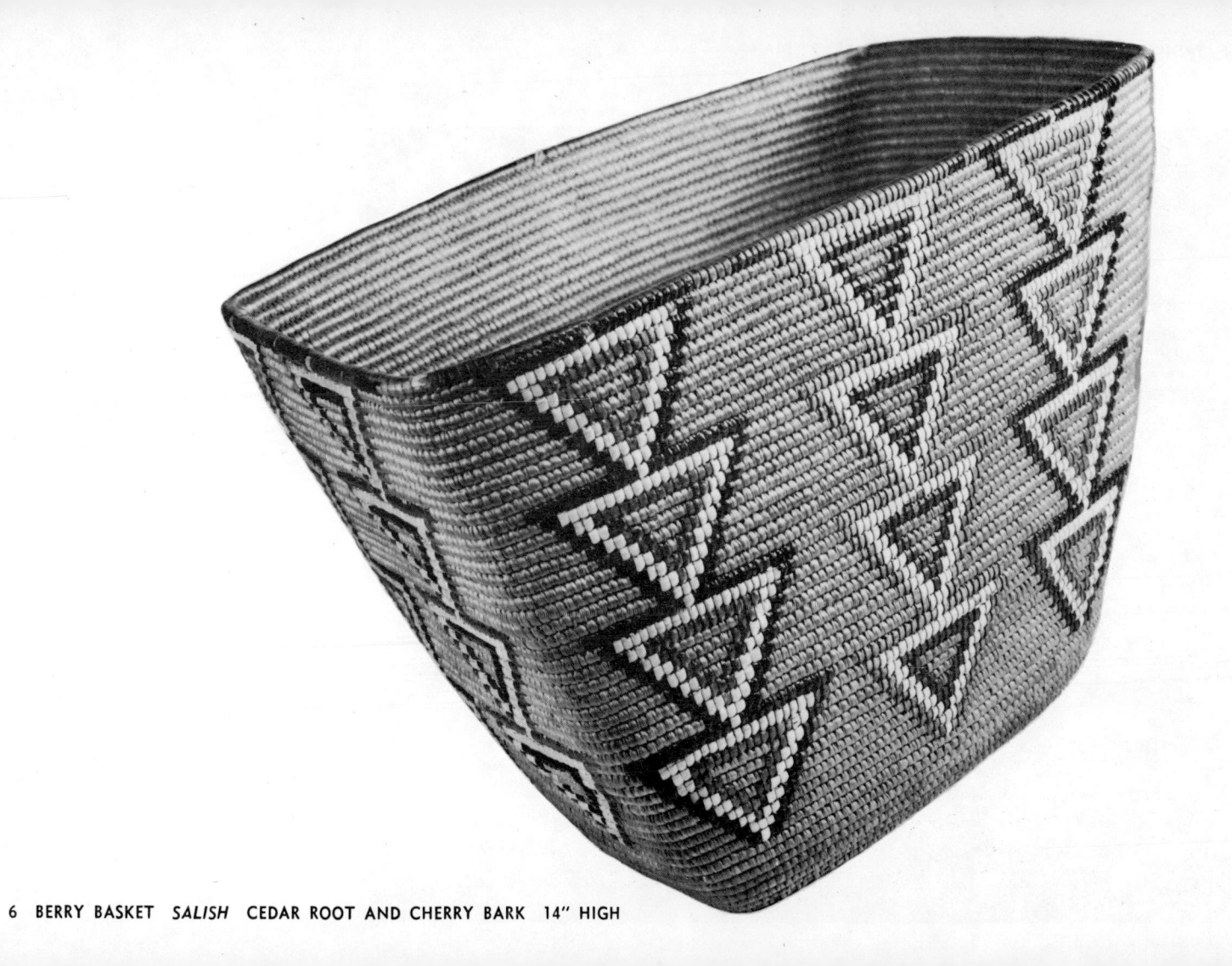

6 BERRY BASKET *SALISH* CEDAR ROOT AND CHERRY BARK 14" HIGH

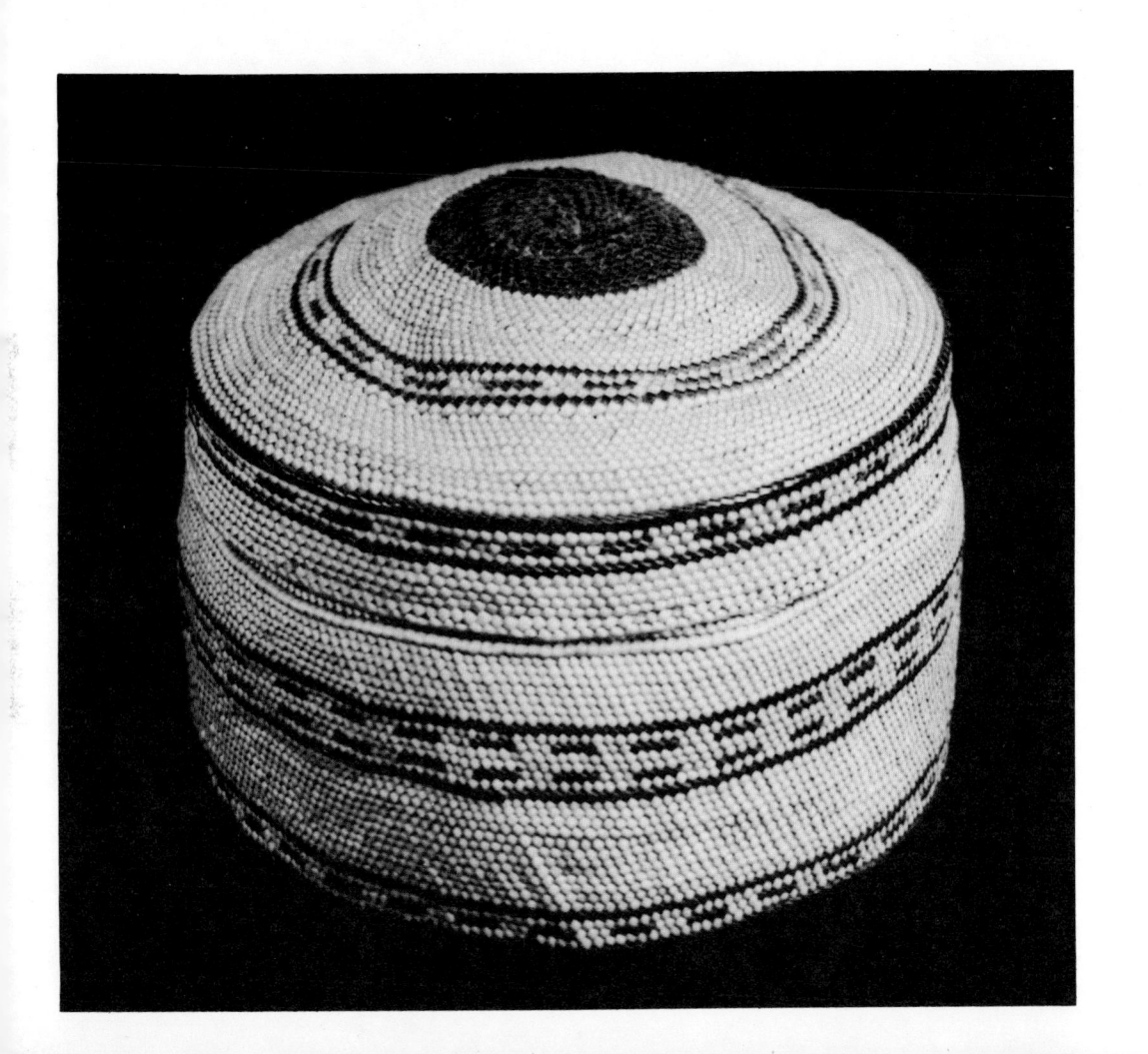

8 BASKET *TLINGIT* SPRUCE ROOT AND DYED FERN 8″ HIGH

10 CLAM BASKET AND DIGGING STICK *KWAKIUTL* STICK 30″ LONG

11 HAT *HAIDA* SPRUCE ROOT, PAINTED 18" DIA.

12 BRACELET *HAIDA* INCISED SILVER 1½" HIGH

14

13

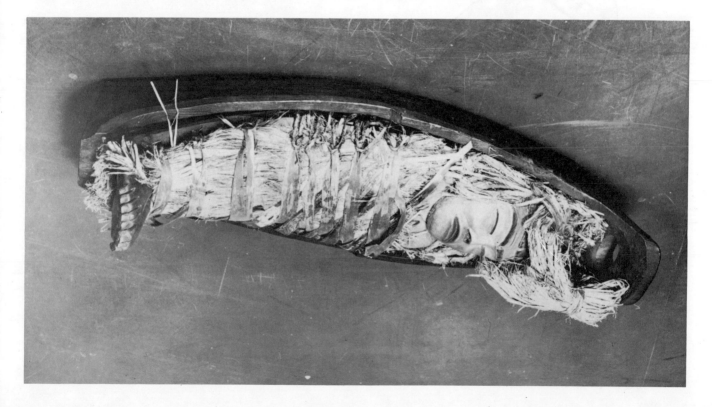

13 MAT CREASERS NOOTKA 5" LONG   14 SALISH 5" LONG →

15 CRADLE WITH HEAD DEFORMING PAD OF CEDAR BARK & FIGURE OF CHILD KWAKIUTL 30" LONG

20 SPOON *HAIDA* MOUNTAIN GOAT HORN 9″ LONG

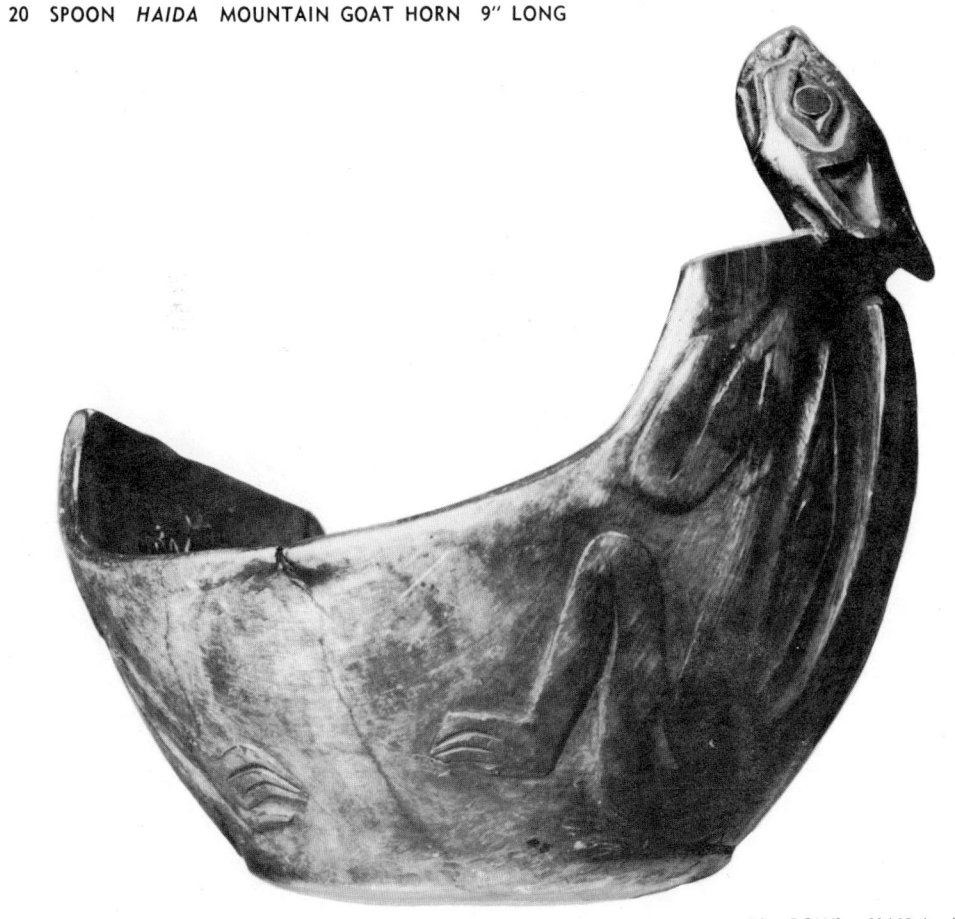

18 BOWL *HAIDA* MOUNTAIN SHEEP HORN 8½″ LONG

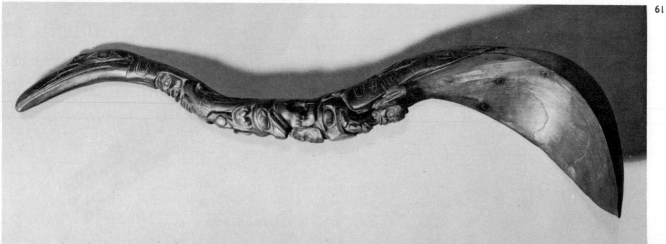

21 LADLE KWAKIUTL CARVED WOOD 2 FT. LONG

23 OIL DISH KWAKIUTL CARVED WOOD 12" LONG

25 CANOE BAILER *TSIMSHIAN* CARVED WOOD 18" LONG

→ 26 SEA-GOING CANOE—NORTHERN TYPE *KWAKIUTL* CEDAR 23½ FT. LONG

27 MODEL WAR CANOE *HAIDA* CARVED WOOD, PAINTED 26" LONG

27

26

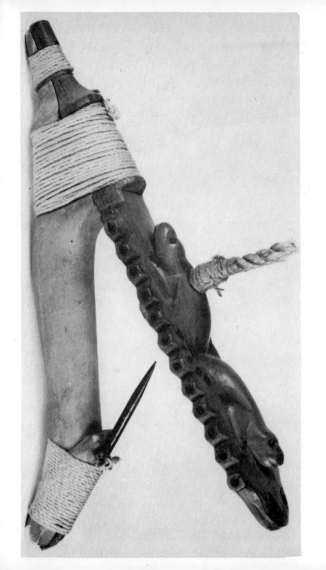

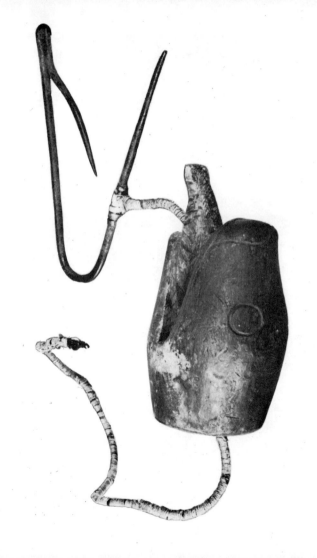

28 HALIBUT HOOK & LURE *HAIDA* CARVED WOOD, IRON HOOK 12" LONG

29 HALIBUT HOOK *KWAKIUTL* CARVED WOOD 10" LONG

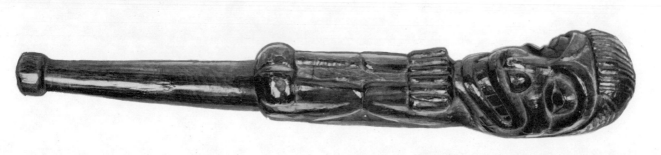

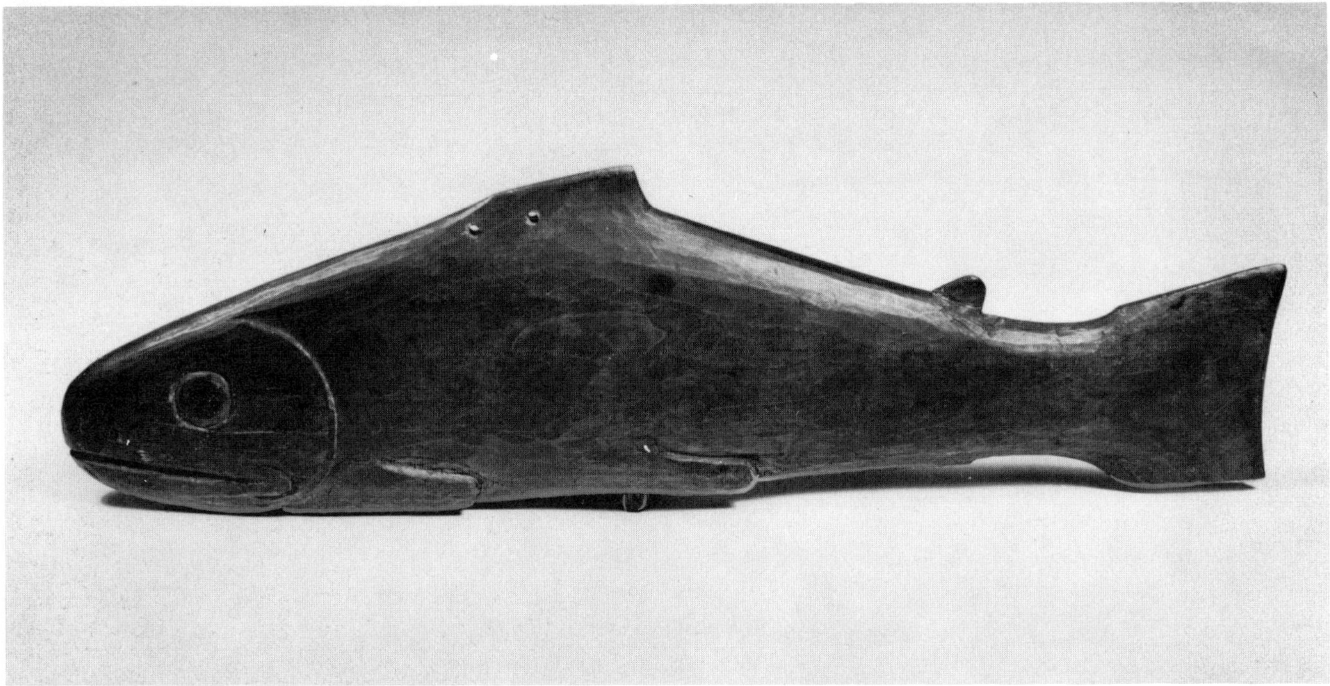

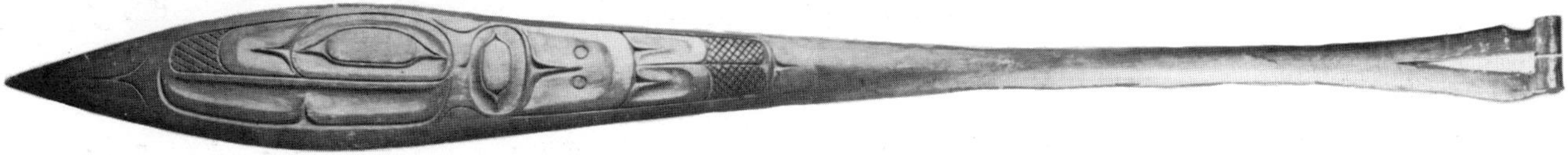

32 SALMON CHARM *KWAKIUTL* CARVED WOOD, PAINTED 12″ LONG

33 PADDLE *TLINGIT* CARVED WOOD 4 FT. LONG

34 DAGGER *TLINGIT* METAL BLADE, WOOD HANDLE INLAID WITH ABALONE 22" LONG

35 MAWL *KWAKIUTL* CARVED STONE 5" DEEP

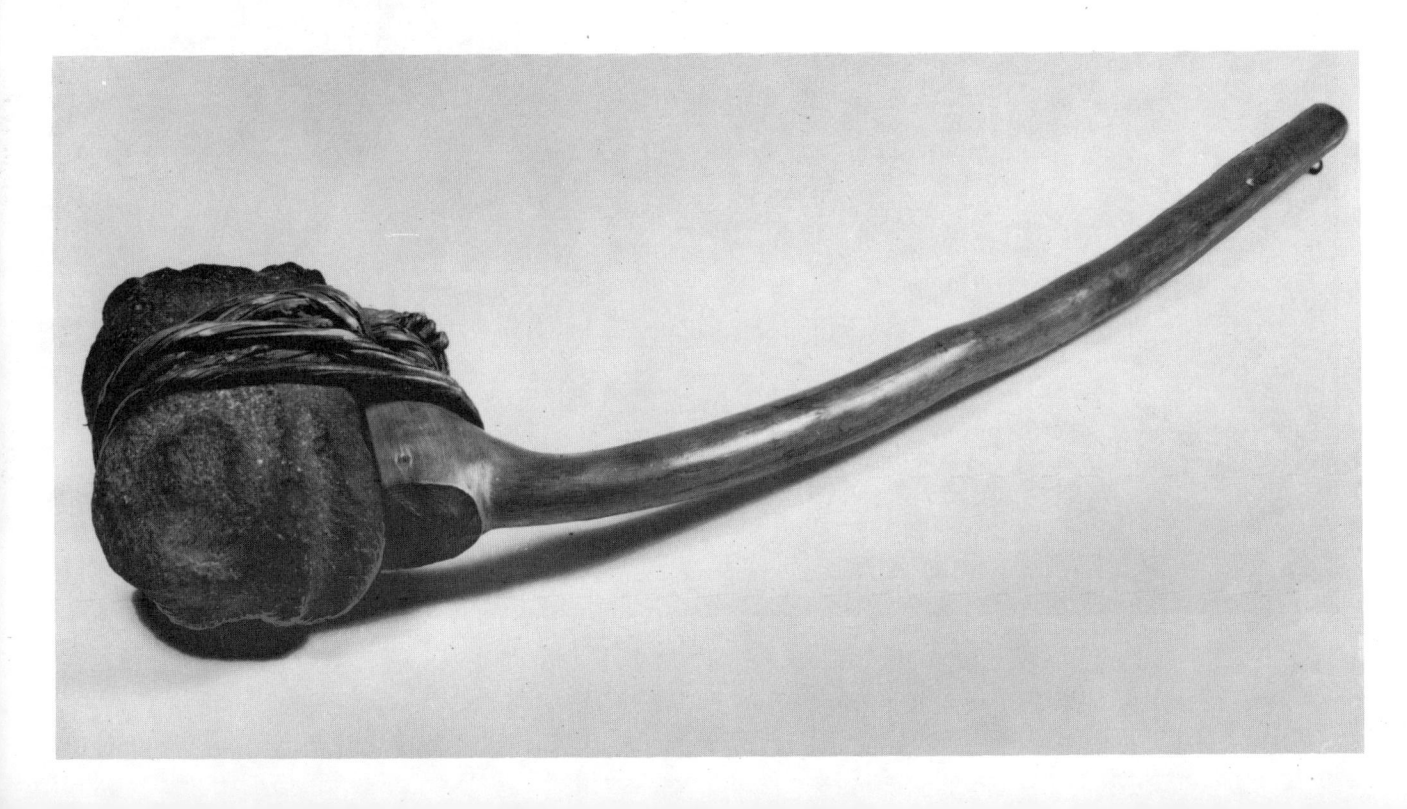

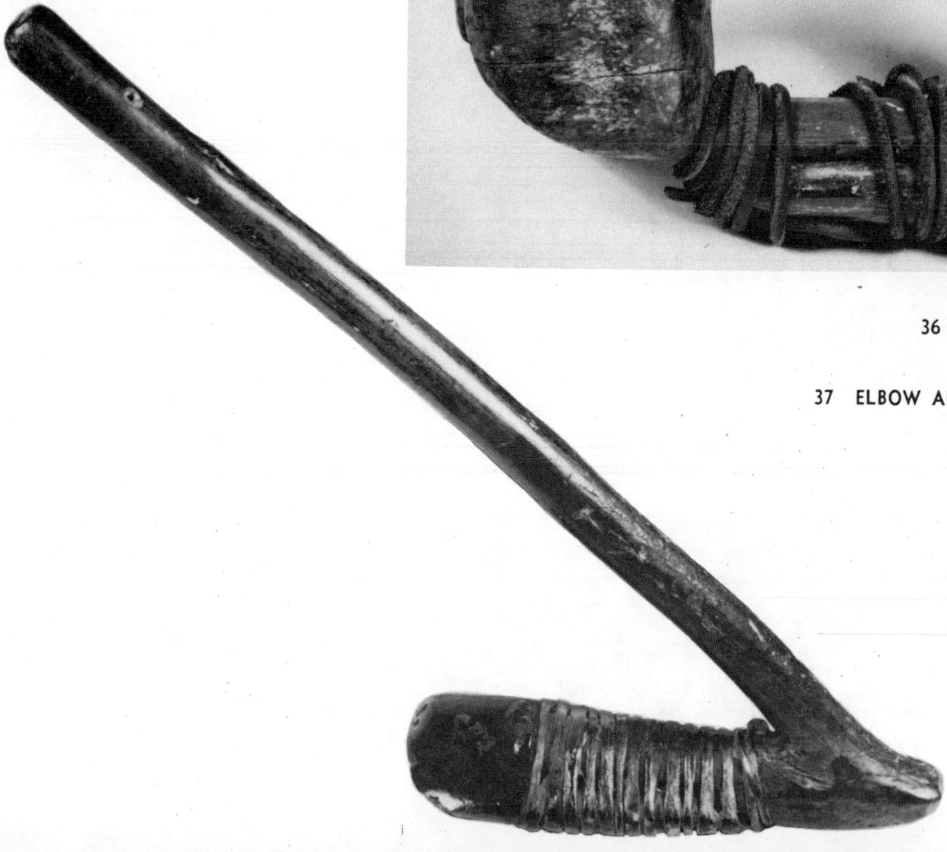

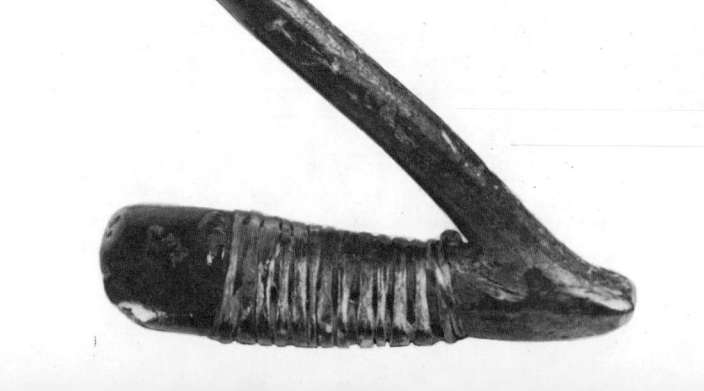

36 "D" ADZE *KWAKIUTL* STONE BLADE 10" LONG

37 ELBOW ADZE *KWAKIUTL* STONE BLADE 5" LONG (BLADE)

38 PILE DRIVER BELLA COOLA STONE 12" HIGH

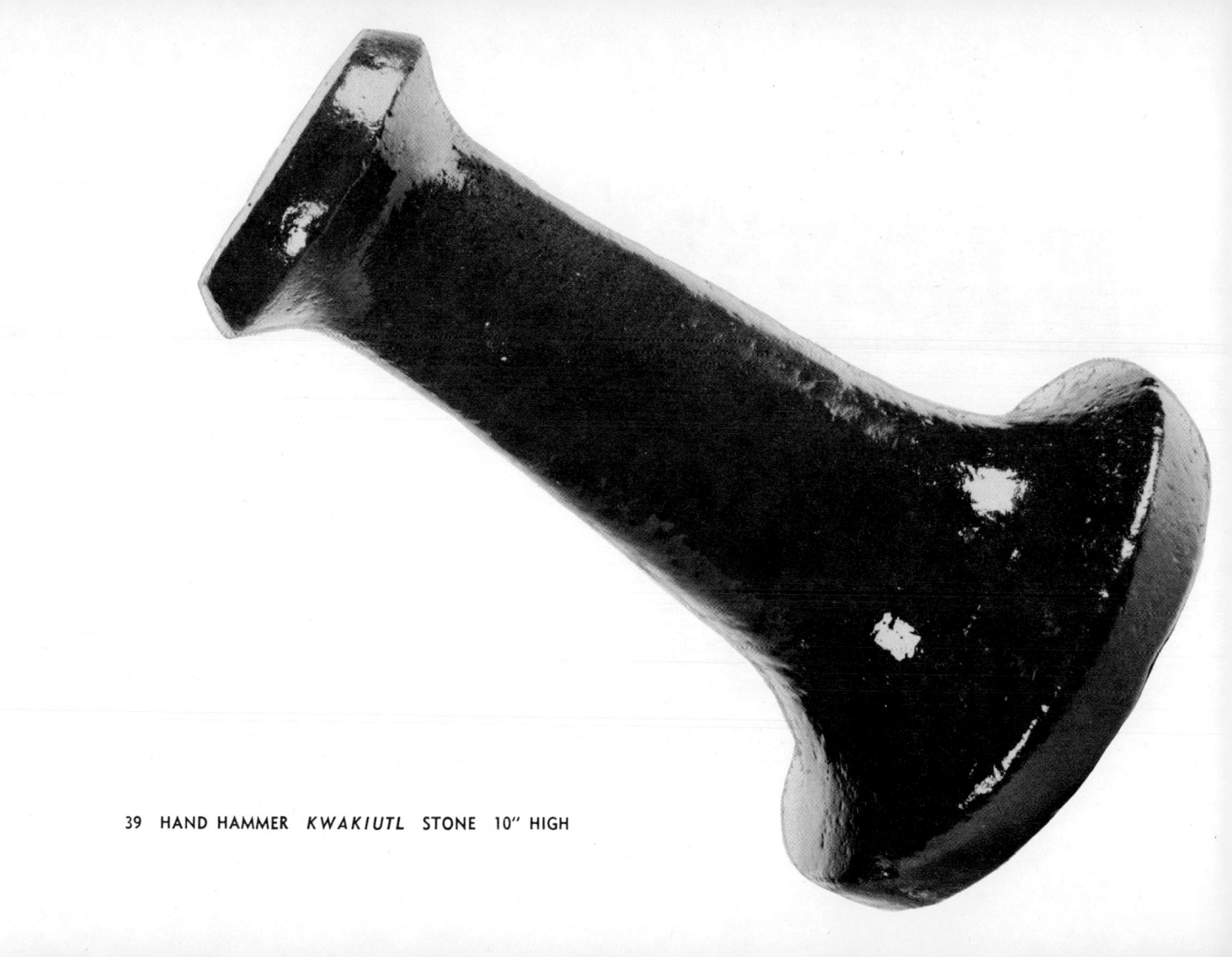

39 HAND HAMMER *KWAKIUTL* STONE 10″ HIGH

40 HUDSON'S BAY MUSKET *HAIDA* CARVED AND CUT DOWN 3 FT. LONG

41 PAINT BRUSH *HAIDA* CARVED WOOD 10½" LONG

42 BLADE KWAKIUTL CARVED STONE 10" LONG

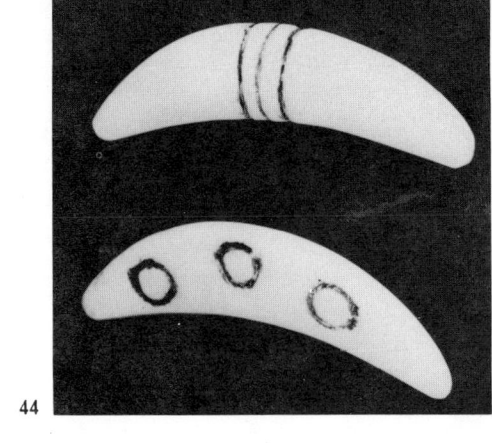

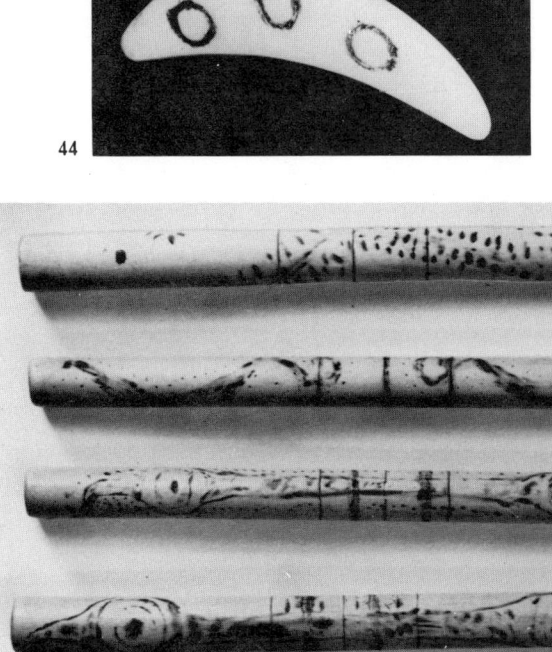

43 GAMBLING STICKS *TSIMSHIAN* WOOD INLAID WITH ABALONE 3½"

44 DICE *KWAKIUTL* INCISED BONE 2"

→ 45 GAMBLING STICKS *TSIMSHIAN* INCISED WOOD, PAINTED 3½"

46 CANOE WITH FIGURES *HAIDA* ARGILLITE 10" LONG

47 FLUTE *HAIDA* ARGILLITE, BONE INLAY 16" LONG

48 TOTEM POLE *TRIBE UNKNOWN* CARVED STONE 10" HIGH

→ 49 TOTEM POLE *HAIDA* ARGILLITE 9" HIGH

52 DETAIL OF TOTEM POLE KWAKIUTL CARVED WOOD, PAINTED

51 GRIZLEY BEAR TOTEM POLE AT TANOO HAIDA CEDAR 30 FT. HIGH

55 HOUSE POST—HUMAN FORM *KWAKIUTL* CARVED WOOD 5 FT. HIGH

→ 56 DETAIL—NOTE ADZE MARKS

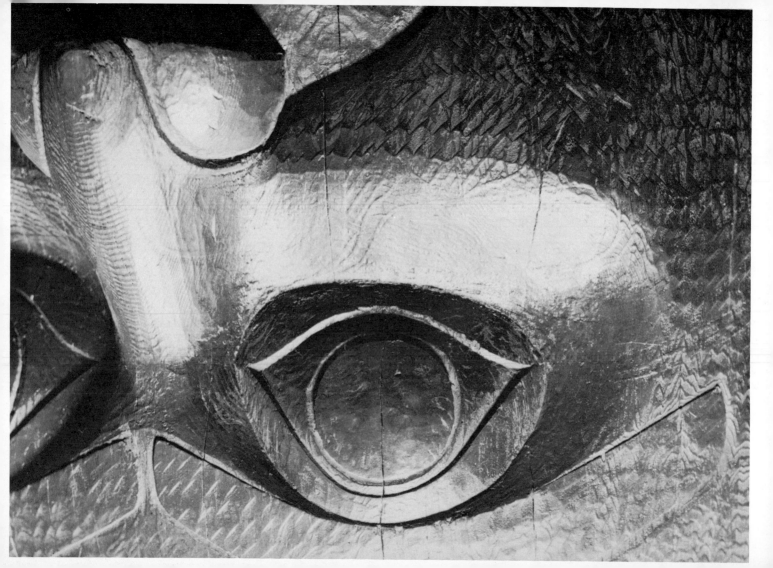

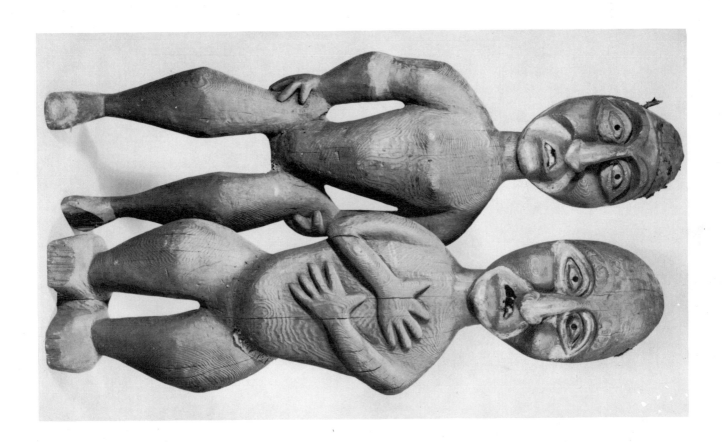

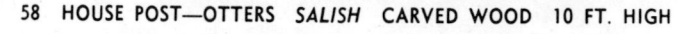

58 HOUSE POST—OTTERS *SALISH* CARVED WOOD 10 FT. HIGH

← 57 MOURNING FIGURES *SALISH* CARVED WOOD 5 FT. HIGH

59 PRE-HISTORIC BOWL CARVED STONE 22" HIGH

60 WOMAN, KILLER WHALE AND SCULPIN *TSIMSHIAN* CARVED STONE 18" HIGH

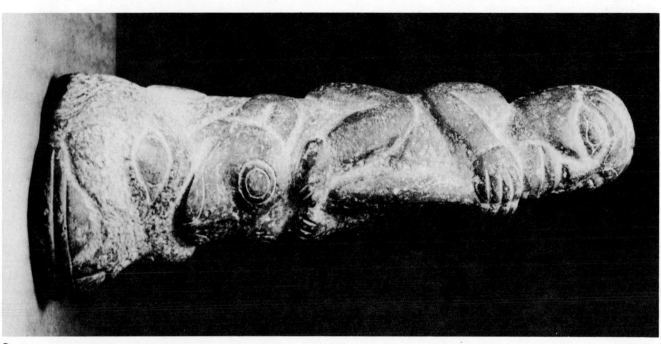

61 MORTAR *HAIDA* CARVED STONE 10" LONG

64   MASK—SKHWAY KHWEY   SALISH   CARVED WOOD 22" HIGH

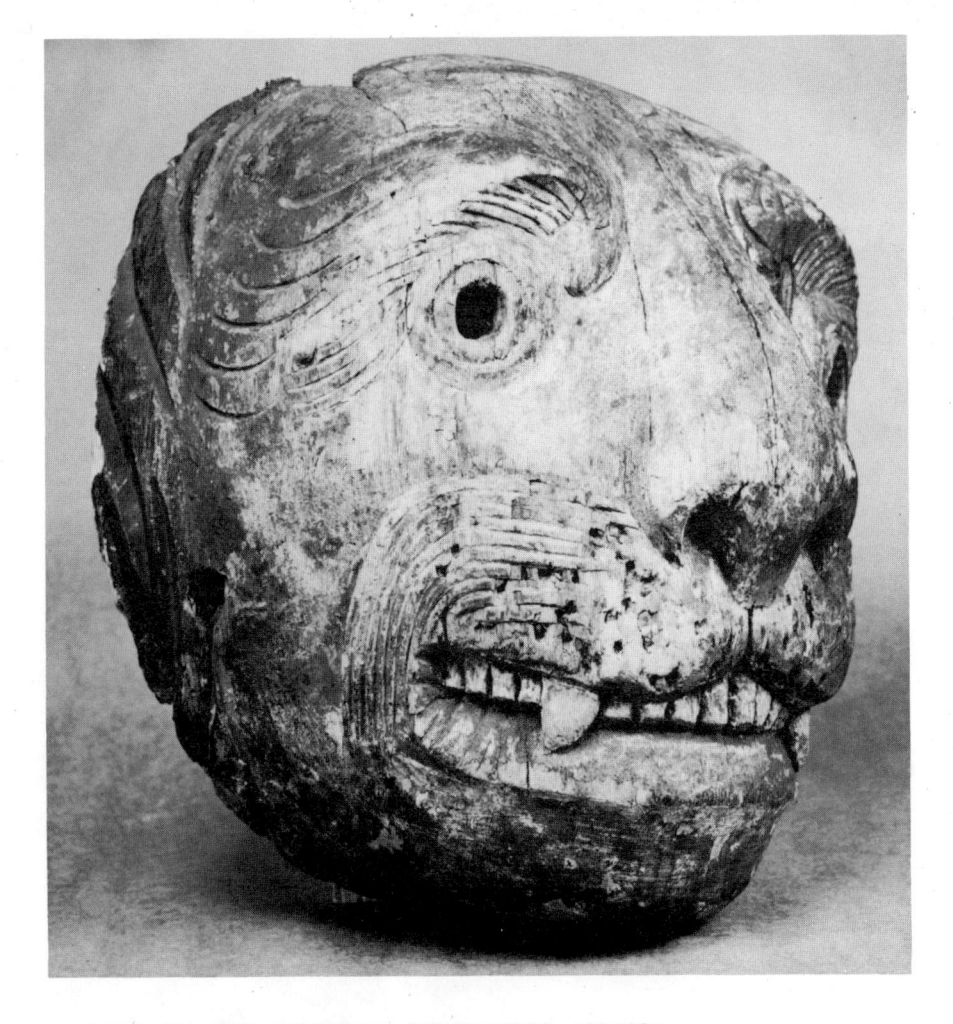

65 MASK—SEA LION *TSIMSHIAN* CARVED WOOD 10″ HIGH

66 SPIRIT MASK *KWAKIUTL* CARVED WOOD 8" HIGH

← 67 MASK—WOMAN *BELLA COOLA* CARVED WOOD, PAINTED 17" HIGH

68 MASK—*TRIBE UNKNOWN* CARVED WOOD, PAINTED 8" HIGH

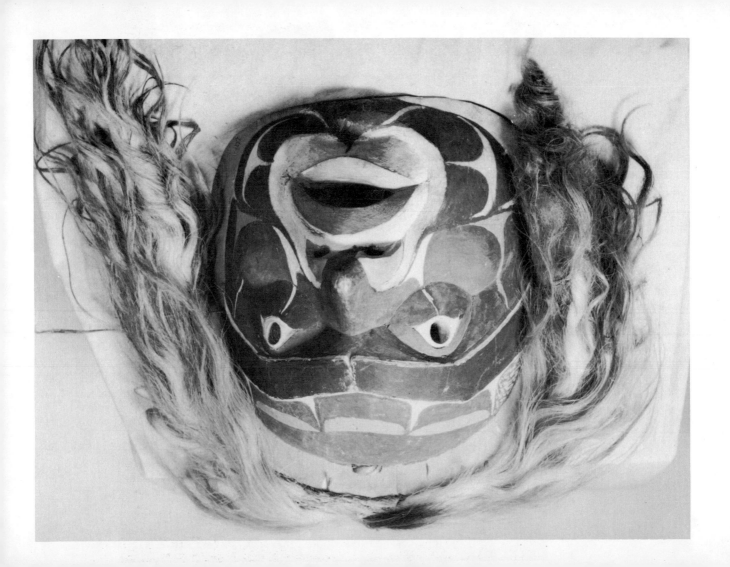

72 MASK—BIRD MONSTER *KWAKIUTL* CARVED WOOD, PAINTED 5 FT. LONG

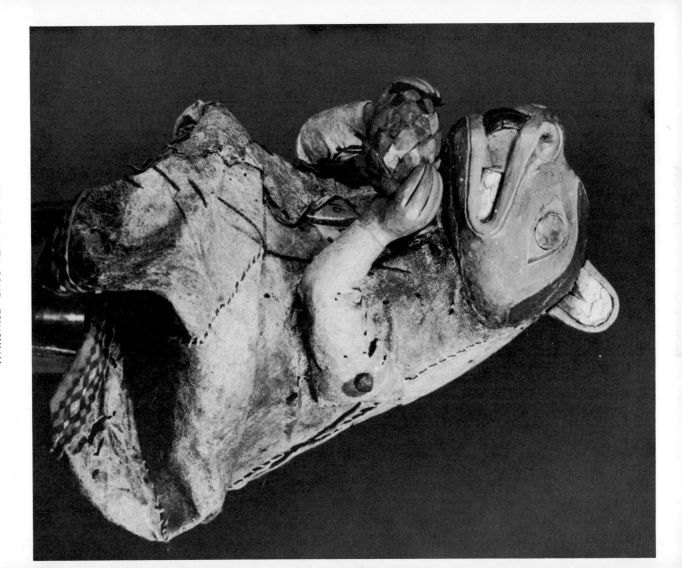

73 CREST OF DANCE HAT—SQUIRREL WITH CONE—*TSIMSHIAN*
CARVED WOOD, PAINTED, ABALONE INLAY AND HIDE 6" HIGH

75 HEADPIECE *KWAKIUTL* CARVED WOOD, PAINTED 4" HIGH

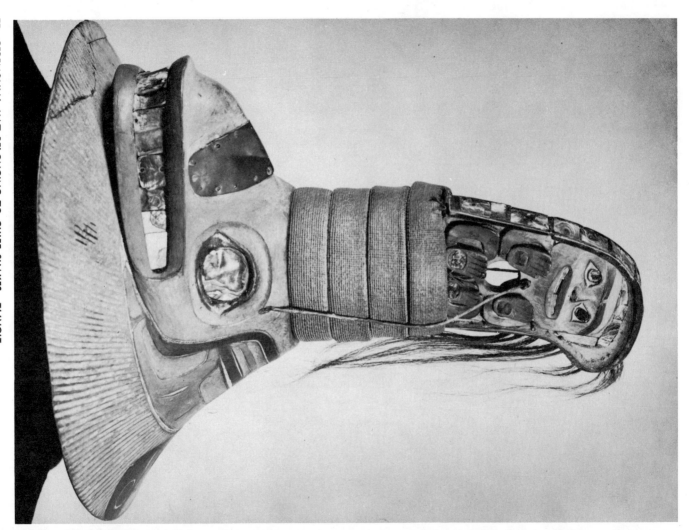

79 CEREMONIAL DAGGER TSONOQUA *KWAKIUTL* CARVED WOOD 15″ LONG

→ 80 WOODEN HELMET—KILLER WHALE CREST *HAIDA* CARVED WOOD, PAINTED, COPPER INLAY 18″ DIA.

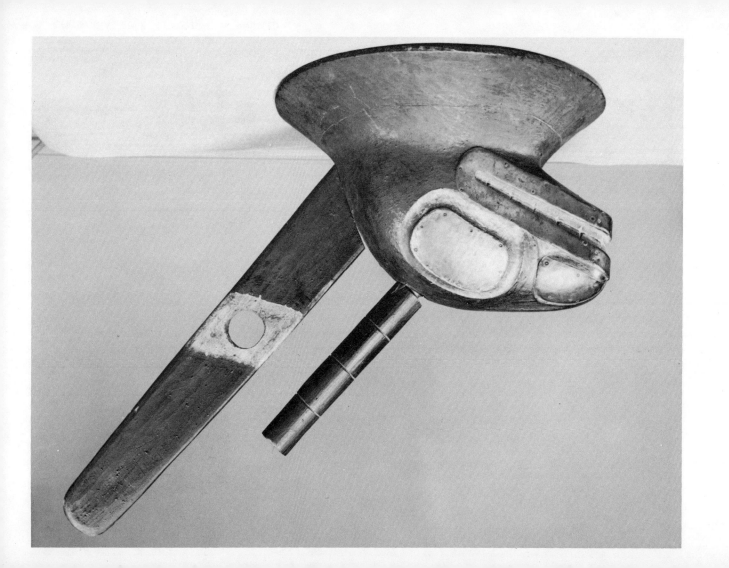

81 CEREMONIAL ROBE *TLINGIT* HIDE, PAINTED

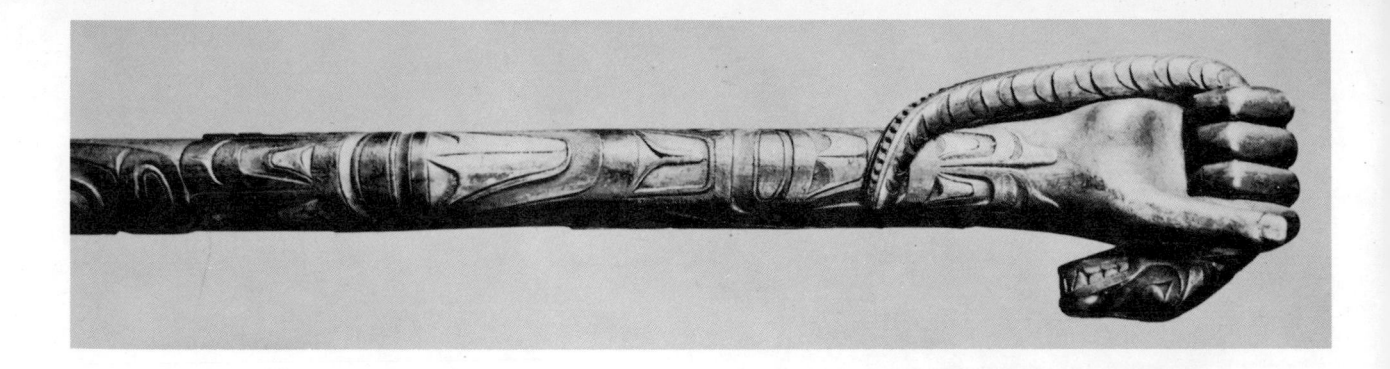

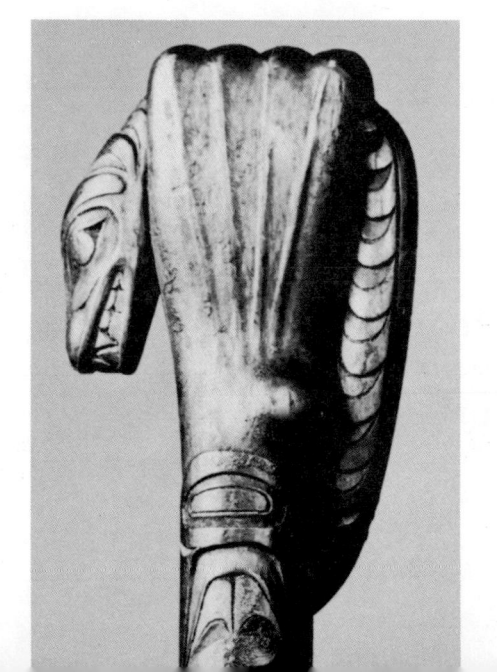

82 CHIEF'S STAFF *HAIDA* CARVED WOOD, PAINTED 35" LONG

84

83

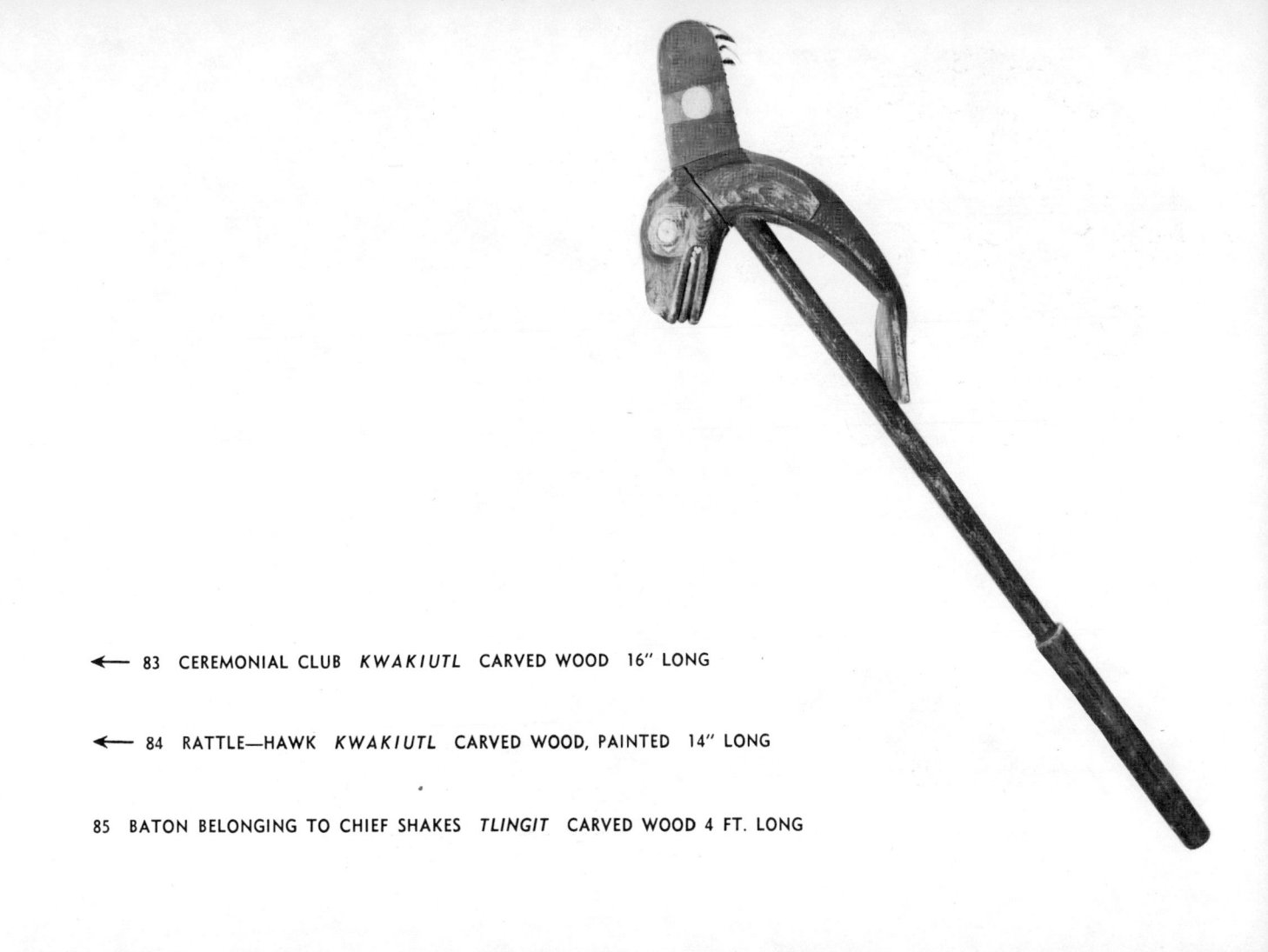

← 83 CEREMONIAL CLUB *KWAKIUTL* CARVED WOOD 16" LONG

← 84 RATTLE—HAWK *KWAKIUTL* CARVED WOOD, PAINTED 14" LONG

85 BATON BELONGING TO CHIEF SHAKES *TLINGIT* CARVED WOOD 4 FT. LONG

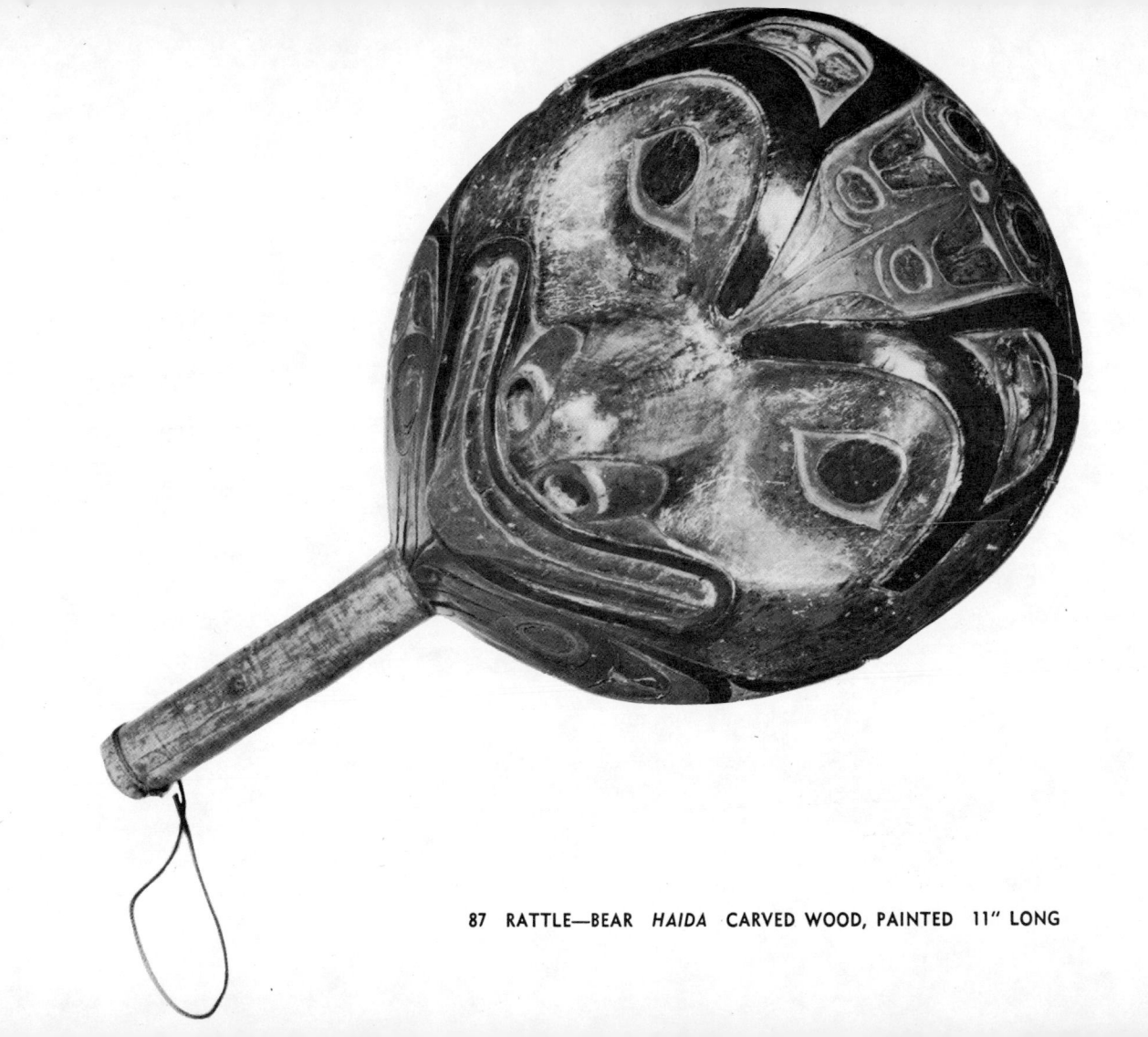

87 RATTLE—BEAR *HAIDA* CARVED WOOD, PAINTED 11" LONG

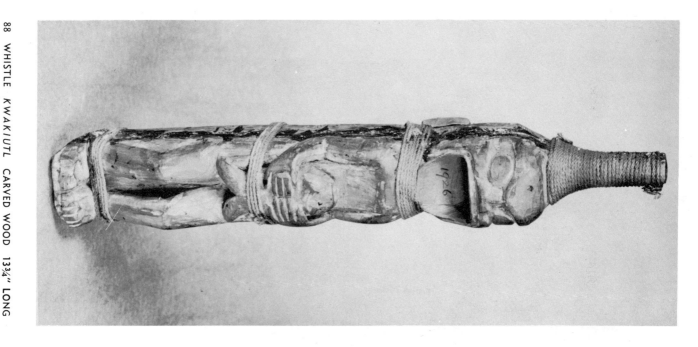

RATTLE *TRIBE UNKNOWN* CARVED WOOD 6¼" WIDE

89

90 CEREMONIAL CURTAIN *KWAKIUTL* PAINTED MUSLIN 10 FT. WIDE

91 DRUM *HAIDA*

DEER HIDE, PAINTED 24" DIA.

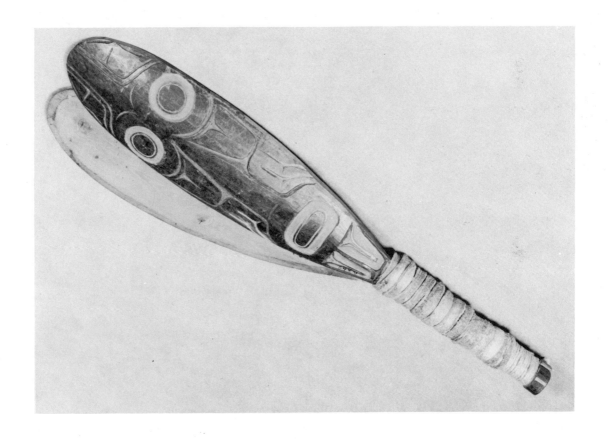

93 CHIEF'S SEAT *HAIDA* CARVED WOOD, PAINTED 51" WIDE

94 TWO-PIECE FEAST DISH *NOOTKA* CARVED WOOD, PAINTED 30" LONG EACH

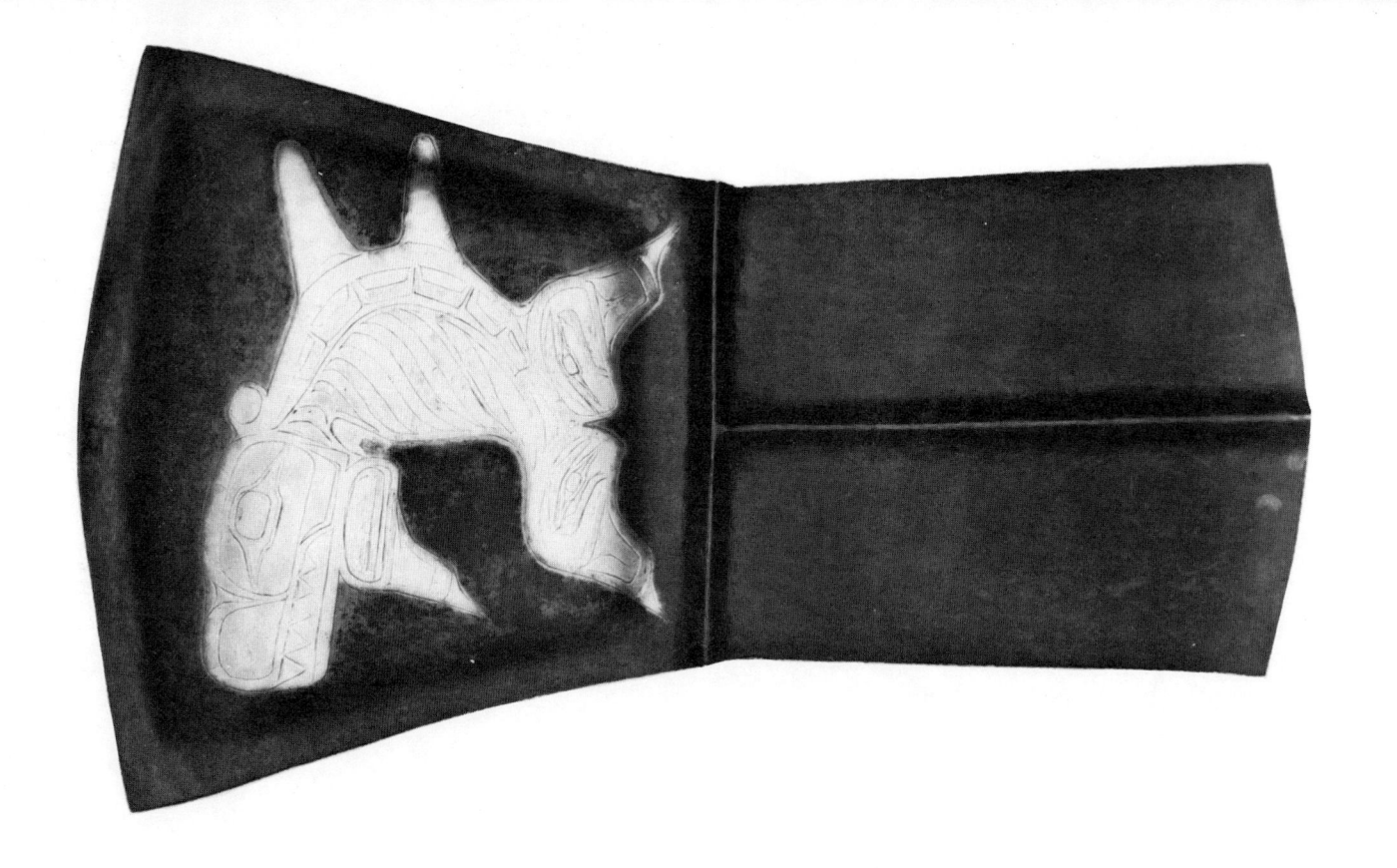

95 POTLATCH COPPER *HAIDA* INCISED COPPER 29¼″ HIGH

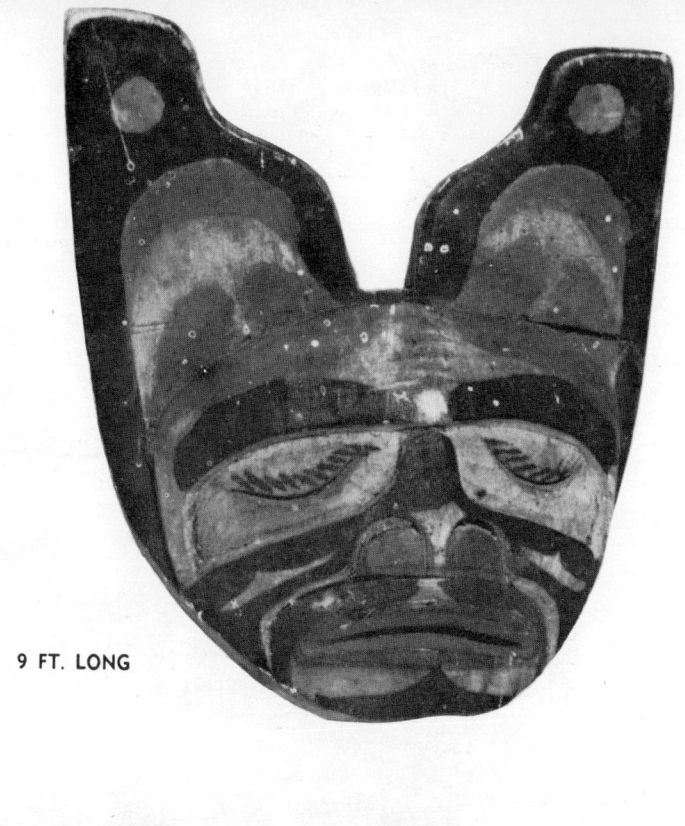

96 HEAD AND TAIL OF HARPOON USED IN COPPER CEREMONY

KWAKIUTL CARVED WOOD, PAINTED, IRON BLADE, MIRROR EYES 9 FT. LONG

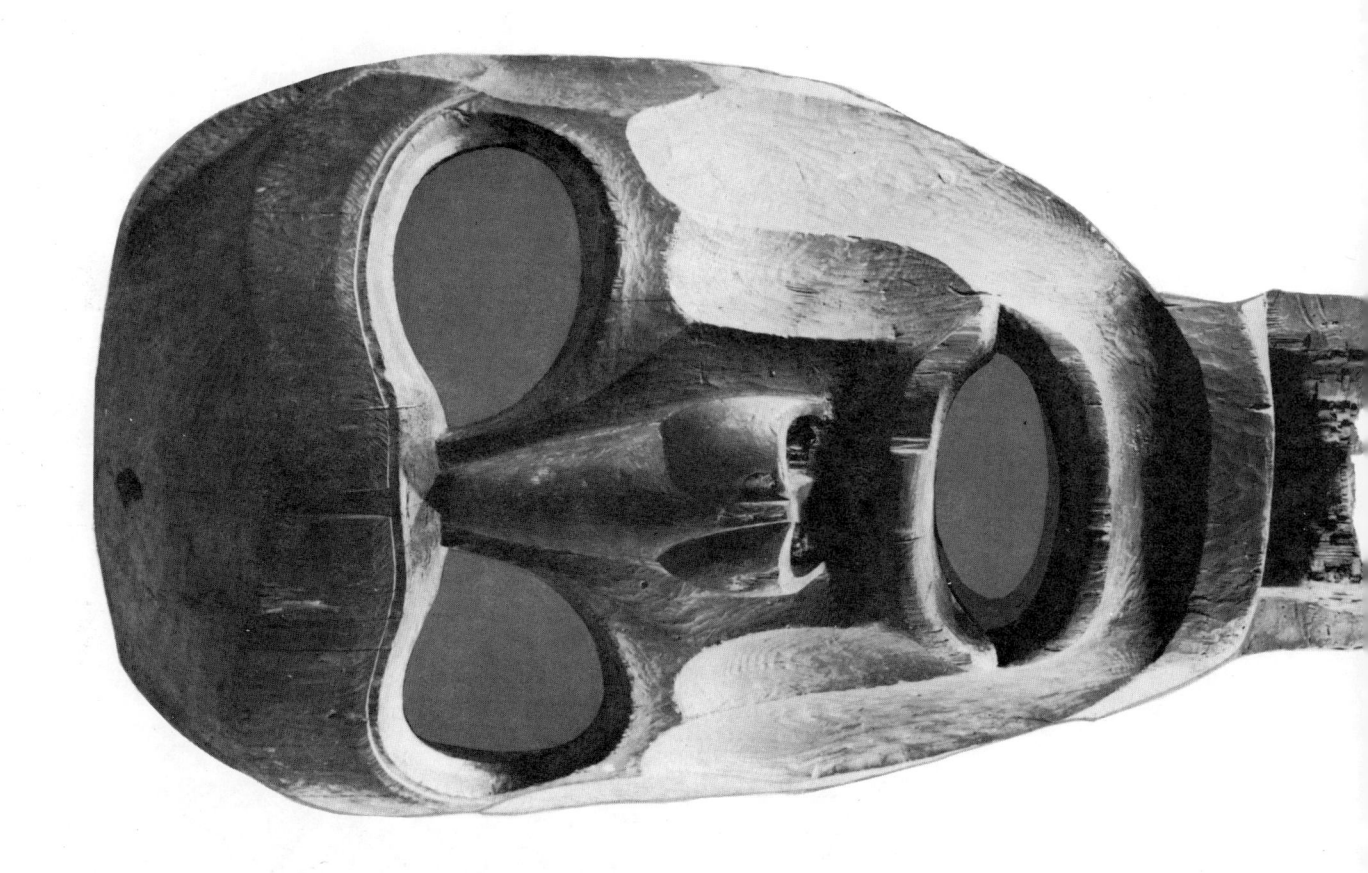

98 FEAST DISH—EAGLE *KWAKIUTL* CARVED WOOD, PAINTED 30" LONG

99 SHAMAN'S CHARM FIGURE *TSIMSHIAN* CARVED WOOD 11½" HIGH

→ 100 DANCE FIGURE *TRIBE UNKNOWN* CARVED WOOD WITH HUMAN HAIR

22" HIGH

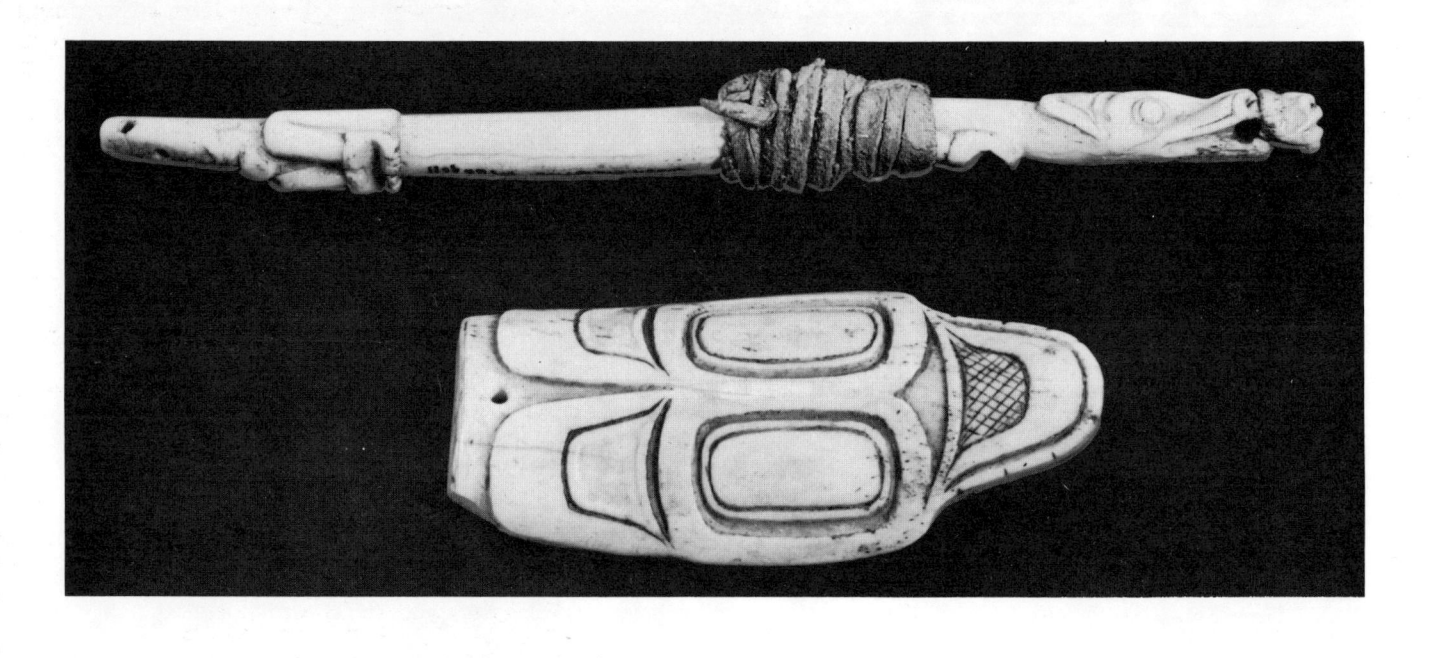

101 CHARMS *TLINGIT* CARVED IVORY 2″ and 4″

→ CHARMS *TSIMSHIAN*

102 MASK BONE 2″ HIGH

103 DUCK BONE 2⅞″ LONG

104 EAGLE STONE 1⅝″ HIGH

104

102

103

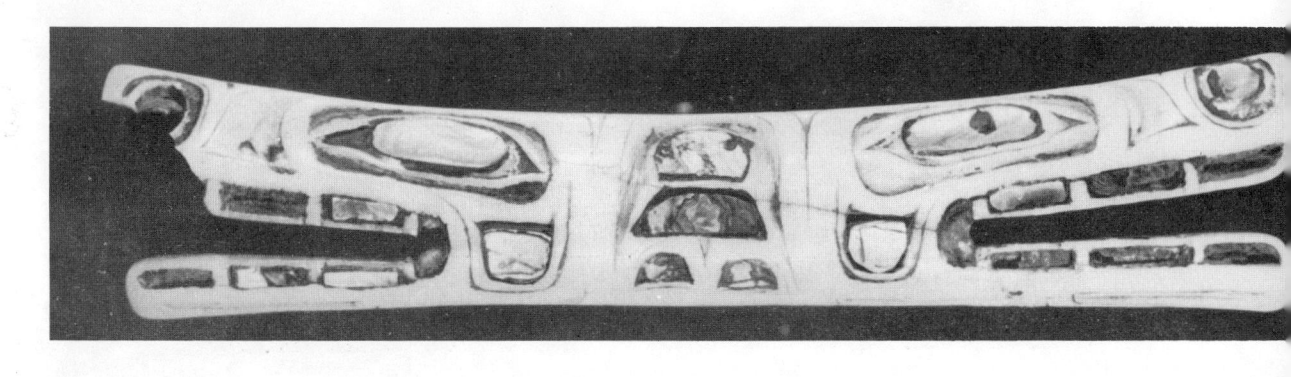

105 SHAMAN'S SOUL CATCHER *KWAKIUTL* CARVED WOOD 7" LONG

106 SHAMAN'S SOUL CATCHER *HAIDA* BONE, ABALONE INLAY 7½" LONG

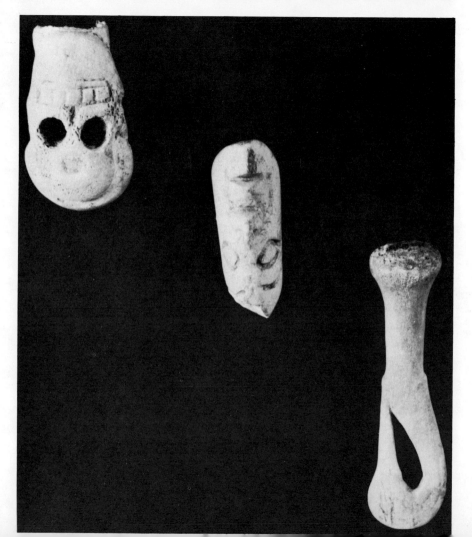

108 CHARM BOX *TLINGIT* CARVED WOOD 18" LONG

109 BURIAL BOX *KWAKIUTL* CARVED WOOD, PAINTED 42" LONG

OAN/OCEANIE-AFRIQUE NOIRE
9 EAST 38TH ST., NY, NY 10016
PHONE 212-779-0486

EVERGREEN PRESS LIMITED